Reclaiming Your Real Self

ISBN 1-4392-2755-1
ISBN 13 978-1439227558

To order additional copies, please contact us.
BookSurge
www.booksurge.com
1-866-308-6235
orders@booksurge.com

Reclaiming Your Real Self

A Psychological and Spiritual Integration

Rick Johnson Ph.D.

2009

Dedication

For Joellyn, Madelyn, and Mia—I rejoice in the connection of our hearts.

For those seeking meaning.

CONTENTS

Chapter 1
An Introduction

"A spiritual life of some kind is absolutely necessary for
psychological health; at the same time, excessive or ungrounded
spirituality can be dangerous, leading to all kinds of compulsive
and even violent behavior."
Thomas Moore, *Care of the Soul*

Most of us spend our first decades closely tied to our unique
family system, with all its positive and challenging aspects. We
do our best to adapt to the particular experiences and circumstances of our families and lives. We develop ideas about what
it means to be happy and successful. We learn, work, play, love,
and experience all that life brings our way, including plenty of
suffering. We spend most of our time doing what we think will
reduce suffering and bring us happiness and approval. Many of
us think that our journey will lead to the attainment of certain
life goals: jobs, material possessions, relationships, and external
accomplishments. Although it often does, sometimes along the
way we can get lost. Our initial visions and plans for happiness
become unsustainable. We lose our sense of meaning and do not
fully inhabit our lives. We lose touch with our inner wisdom and
intuitive clarity. As a result, our definitions of health and success
need to be modified.

A sustainable life journey must travel back to you, to your
core self. The core of our being is what I refer to as the Real Self,
a term coined by Karen Horney, a post-Freudian psychoanalyst.

Rick Johnson Ph.D.

The Real Self contains our potentials for growth and creativity as well as our wisdom about what is life-affirming and life-enhancing for us. It is our *inner guide* to healing, growth, abundance, and the potential for transcendence. We really do know what is good for us; we simply forget, don't listen, or look in the wrong places. Thus, we get lost.

A variety of psychological theories and approaches, like Karen Horney's, espouse the idea that we have inner wisdom available to us. In Chapter Two I summarize some of these key theories to illustrate a convergence of ideas and to set the stage for an integrative view of healing and growth. Although they point to the existence of a foundational sense of being within all of us, the Real Self, psychological theories typically fall short of addressing the spiritual aspects of healthy living.

In fact, psychology and spirituality have historically had difficulty co-existing. The disconnect between psychological approaches and spirituality has many roots, with entrenched beliefs from each side contributing to the rift. Generally speaking, psychological practitioners have tended to ignore and minimize spiritual aspects of living while spiritual practitioners have viewed psychological interventions as unnecessary in the face of faith and spiritual practice.

This rift is unfortunate, but to some degree changing. Movements in the field of psychology, such as pastoral counseling, transpersonal psychology, body oriented therapies, mind-body medicine, positive psychology, and Buddhist psychology, are speaking to people who are interested in learning about various forms of integrative, reflective practice. This movement toward integration has also been supported by spiritual practitioners as the definition of spirituality has been broadened and clarified as potentially distinct from organized religion. This broadening has engendered a more inclusive view of spirituality that is sparking interest in many who have felt unrepresented by and reactive to organized religion.

Because the topic of spirituality is a very personal one for many people, I have chosen to talk about spirituality very broadly and inclusively in the hopes that every reader can work within their own faith structure and utilize their own personal definition and views of spirituality as they consider the concepts that I present. Various ways of defining, experiencing and accessing spirituality are elaborated upon in Chapter Three and throughout the book.

I believe that the Real Self contains not only psychological wisdom, but also our spiritual potential. The Real Self has the capacity to connect to a larger source, the source from which we all originate. The Real Self is the conduit through which we can touch the divine and cultivate growthful, loving, abundant, and sustainable energy in our lives. When we are disconnected from the Real Self we are psychologically and spiritually lost. By accessing and experiencing spirituality in our lives, we develop our personal integrity and refine our wisdom about what is life-affirming for us. When we make decisions based upon our personal integrity, our choices reflect our core values and engender sustainable meaning.

The consequences of being out of contact with your Real Self and associated spirituality can be severe. Although suffering is an inevitable and ultimately useful part of living, nagging feelings of restlessness, meaninglessness, and emptiness—common precipitators for people to enter psychotherapy—are signals sent to your consciousness from your body and soul. They are signaling a disconnect between the wisdom and spiritual grounding of your Real Self and your actual life. When your life choices, relationships, and activities are not congruent with your Real Self and associated integrity, your suffering will increase. Conditions such as depression, anxiety, chronic pain, and resentment are a few of the likely outcomes of chronically living your life based on anything other than your own core values, aspirations, and integrity. What occurs is a psychological and spiritual crisis.

Consider these examples:

- Individuals who drag themselves to work each day; their job is a chore rather than a calling; they feel passionless and robotic; they are bored, depressed and unfulfilled; they are at-risk for engaging in affairs or other impulsive behaviors in an attempt to feel alive.

- Individuals who overwork and are disinterested in their primary relationships; they tend to be disconnected from their own and others' emotions; underneath the veneer of their achievement orientation lies fears of inadequacy; they are prone to self-absorption and failed relationships.

- Stay-at-home parents who define their lives solely through their kids; they are exhausted and have lost the sense of who they are; their sense of adult fun and identity are missing.

- Individuals who are in a lifeless and constricted marriage or relationship; they try to restrict their aspirations and desires to avoid disapproval from their spouse/partner; they use various means to distract themselves from their own feelings of disappointment and regret; they may experience chronic anxiety and periodic panic as well as headaches and other kinds of physical pain.

- Individuals who are missing a philosophical and

spiritual grounding; their lives lack meaning, purpose and depth; they may be prone to depression and feelings of alienation and disconnection.

- Individuals who suffer with addictions such as alcohol, drugs, eating, shopping, or pornography; they continuously cycle through indulgence, guilt, and self-loathing; they feel out-of-control and victimized by life and their own addictive behaviors.

- Individuals whose central life-theme is about pleasing or saving others; their self-esteem is based upon the approval of others; they lack a sense of personal power and periodically experience feelings of emptiness, worthlessness, and shame.

- Individuals who are unresolved and out-of-touch with past trauma such as physical or sexual abuse; they distract themselves with activities and tasks to avoid reminders of the trauma; they may experience low self-esteem, chronic anxiety as well as periodic, debilitating panic.

- Individuals who acknowledge and adopt only a socially accepted persona; on the surface they appear well-adjusted; the less socially desirable aspects of their personality are denied and disowned; they may be the first to judge others while concealing their own unintegrated, *shadow side*.

- Individuals who externalize blame and have a need to control others or their life circumstances; they may feel superior to others and chronically frustrated; they are prone to anger and reactivity.

- Individuals who detach themselves from life and relationships; they are spectators in their own life; they tend to restrict their aspirations, desires, and ambitions to avoid being disappointed; they are prone to depression and isolation.

The common denominator across all these examples is that these individuals are out-of-touch with the inner wisdom and clarity of their Real Self. They are disconnected from their intuitive knowing about what is right for them on a soul level. They are experiencing emptiness through restriction of their potentials and often grasp outside themselves in an attempt to fill a void in their life. They quite likely experienced events in their lives that led them to compensate and triggered them into survival mode. Consequently, they stopped listening to their Real Self. As one client recently told me about her family up-bringing, "I just had to survive, but *I* got lost." She was so busy trying to survive and adapt to her difficult life circumstances that she lost touch with her Real Self. When we lose touch with our Real Self and associated spirituality, we lose our inner compass and our most significant source of knowledge and guidance. Chapters Four and Five are devoted to exploring the psychological and spiritual reasons and consequences for losing touch with our Real Self.

So, what happens when we embrace our Real Self? There is actually a fair amount of clinically-informed research that answers this question. In Chapter Six I provide a description of the characteristics of psychologically healthy individuals and the processes that contribute to their health. These characteristics focus on healthy interpersonal boundaries, that is, the ability to connect with others without losing our own sense of self, and include: a balanced sense of personal responsibility, a balance of thoughts and emotional processes, low levels of psychological reactivity, the ability to self-soothe in the face of anxiety and stress, clear inner-generated convictions, direct communication in relationships, confidence in our abilities to meet our needs, and a strong, life-affirming sense of personal integrity.

Chapter Seven builds upon the discussion of psychological health by including spirituality. In particular, spiritual practice assists in the development of personal integrity, which is the voice and consciousness of the Real Self. In Chapter Six I elaborate on key steps that support awareness of the Real Self and associated spiritual wisdom: (a) awakening to spirituality, (b) cultivating personal integrity, (c) evaluating life-structures, and (d) remembering and committing to spiritual practice.

Many people are able to make some amount of change in their lives, only to fall back in old patterns. How can positive change be sustainable? How can spiritual practice support life-affirming values, choices and behaviors without becoming restrictively moralistic? How can psychological and spiritual views of the self be reconciled and integrated? How can psychotherapeutic healing and growth be supported by spiritual practice? The final three chapters of the book tackle these questions.

In Chapter Eight, sustainability of a moral vision is linked to the idea that we need to recognize and embrace all of who we are, not just the socially acceptable parts. Remaining unaware of the parts of ourselves that we attempt to banish from our consciousness is a recipe for acting out in ways that will conflict with our personal integrity. All parts of ourselves will seek expression, even ones that are incongruent with a rigid view of what is acceptable and permissible. So, our personal integrity must include a realistic, holistic, and sustainable view of who we are.

In Chapter Nine I discuss a philosophical and practical integration of psychological and spiritual views of the self. In particular, faith traditions, especially Eastern ones, tend to emphasize ideas of selflessness while psychology tends to help people define and build a stronger sense of self. This chapter focuses on how we can embrace our Real Self, including healthy psychological boundaries, as well as practices based on notions of interconnectedness and selflessness, by incorporating a larger sense of meaning while being true to ourselves.

In Chapter Ten I address how spiritually-oriented psychotherapy can assist us to function more effectively in our lives and reclaim our connection with our Real Self. I discuss an approach that integrates various psychological models with spiritual themes and practices. The approach takes into account research that highlights the factors which account for psychotherapeutic change, including client variables and the alliance between the client and therapist. The focus is on how we can use spiritually-oriented psychotherapy or counseling to support our health and healing.

Why this Book?

Obviously, I believe that an integration of psychology and spirituality has great value for people interested in growth in their lives. Although criticisms of this integration are not without merit, I have increasingly come to believe that the division between spiritually and psychology is unnecessary and often problematic. My work with clients has taught me that growth and healing are most likely to occur when psychological and spiritual practices are combined or integrated. I believe that an integration of psychology and spirituality provides enormous potential to heal wounds and to further individual development as well as human evolution. My own life and my work as a psychotherapist have been wonderfully enriched through the inclusion of various forms of spiritual practice.

Although there are several conceptual options related to

an integration of psychology and spirituality currently available, I believe this book fills a gap by providing an inclusive and accessible view of spirituality as well as a practical approach to integrating the two. It builds upon the strengths of existing psychological theories and approaches, which seem to point to the existence of the Real Self. The audience for this book is anyone interested in emotional, psychological, relational, and spiritual growth. This includes counselors and psychotherapists as well as spiritual practitioners who are interested in a practical integration of psychology and spirituality for themselves and their clients.

The purpose of this book, then, is to provide a practical framework for understanding and attaining psychological and spiritual health. It won't provide easy answers on how to accomplish this, however; but because I believe each of us already possess the knowledge of what is congruent with our soul, my hope is that this book will help readers to remember, reconnect with, and activate their Real Self. The approach in this book will provide a homecoming for many people. As one client said, "It's like I already knew it; I just had to remember." I believe that we all have this inner knowing; we simply have to remember its existence and listen to its voice. It is available every moment.

Chapter 2
Psychological Theories and the Real Self

"The *real self*—that central inner force, common to all human beings and yet unique in each, which is the deep source of growth."
Karen Horney, *Neurosis and Human Growth*

Why do I feel disconnected in my life? Why do I feel depressed and anxious when everything seems to be fine? Why do I react to situations and people the way that I do? Why do I seem to repeat relationship patterns in my life? How can I heal from past traumatic events and relationships? How do I cultivate meaning in my life? Do I have free will in my life? What role do childhood experiences play in my current life? How can I feel less stuck in my life?

Countless psychological theories have been developed in an attempt to provide answers and solutions to questions like these. In this chapter I will briefly summarize some key theories and approaches in the psychotherapy field. My belief is that these theories point to the existence of a foundational sense of being within all of us, the Real Self, which when activated will promote growth, clarity, and happiness and will be a compassionate and wise guide in our lives.

My goal in this chapter is not an exhaustive summary of

available counseling theories, nor is it an in-depth discussion of any particular theory. Rather, I hope to provide an introduction to the key concepts of several theories to illustrate a convergence of ideas and to set the stage for an integrative view of healing and growth. Because Freud's voluminous writings are foundational for many important ideas that subsequent theorists attempted to refute or extend, his theory is a good starting point.

Psychoanalysis: Freud

Not long ago a graduate student stopped by my office, and after seeing a Sigmund Freud Action Figure that previous students had given to me, commented: "You can't really think that Freud has anything worthwhile to contribute to modern psychology." Her objections centered mainly on his largely deterministic views, his focus on the psychosexual stages, and the power imbalance in the client-therapist relationship. Although I agree with some of the criticism of Freud, I find many aspects of his theory to be extremely helpful in my work with clients: namely his view that the personality consists of competing structures, his insights related to defense mechanisms, and his discovery of the repetition compulsion.

Freud proposed that the personality consists of three intrapsychic structures: the id, ego and superego. The id is the primary source of motivation and energy in the personality, the energy being instinctual and expressed mostly through sexual and aggressive drives. The id lives by the pleasure principle and lacks the ability to delay gratification. The ego is the manager of the personality and operates by the reality principle. It manages the immature and irrational impulses of the id and deals with the demands of the external world, including the superego. The superego represents our moral training and develops when we internalize the standards of society. The superego is driven by the perfection principle. The demands of the superego often clash with the id's instinctual needs, which creates anxiety for us. As an example, imagine yourself standing in front of an open refrigerator and looking at a piece of chocolate cake. Your id says, "Go for it." Your superego says, "Don't do it. Remember your diet." Your ego says, "Ok, you can have just a small piece, but you'll have to wait until after a healthy dinner."

The ego copes with the conflict between the id and superego and the inevitable anxiety that the conflict generates by using of a variety of defense mechanisms, with repression being the most prominent defense in Freud's theory. Repression protects the ego from anxiety by unconsciously excluding threatening and painful thoughts from conscious awareness. So, when the id's demands are too outlandish or intense in comparison to the superego's standards, the ego jumps to our rescue by using a defense mechanism such as repression.

The previous example of the chocolate cake provides an illustration of how the defense process works. What happens if your id's demands overwhelm your ego's attempt at a rational solution and you grabbed the cake and stuff it into your mouth? Most likely, you would employ a defense mechanism to protect the ego from the anxiety that would result from this action. Repression or its more conscious side-kicks, denial and rationalization, may become activated. You may hear yourself saying phrases like, "That wasn't such a big of a piece of cake. I deserve it. I'll simply skip desert. I'll easily burn off those calories while I sleep!"

Another aspect of Freud's theory I find particularly helpful in my work is what he called the *repetition compulsion*: the term used to describe the tendency to repeat certain situations and relationships that were unresolved or troublesome from childhood. In other words, people have a tendency to repeat painful situations and relationships again and again, such as being attracted to the same type of intimate partner, even when it continues to work out badly. This dynamic is often baffling and infuriating when we watch it occur in others and in ourselves. As one client remarked, "I must be a creep magnet. I keep attracting the same type of creepy guy over and over." In this case, my client was attracted to men that reminded her, albeit unconsciously, of her narcissistic and unavailable father. Although Freud never fully explained this phenomenon, only saying that the intense pain of the original situation causes people to fixate on it, other theorists have provided more useful explanations of this dynamic, which is so important in our attempts to heal and grow in our lives.

Jung's Analytic Theory

Carl Jung, a contemporary of Freud, proposed ideas that broke radically from traditional Freudian thought by focusing on what could be termed psychoanalytic mysticism. Jung believed that religion held more healing and redemptive power than did psychological analysis alone. Many people consider him to be the pioneer of the integration of psychology and spirituality. His work continues to grow in popularity and is currently well represented by James Hollis, among others. Jung's theory is vast and comprehensive, with several key concepts being important to this book, including his ideas about the structure of the personality and our ability to connect to transcendent experience and knowledge.

For Jung, the ego is the center of our consciousness. It is the totality of our conscious being: our memories, thoughts, feelings, and sensory perceptions. Like Freud, he argued that each of us has a personal unconscious which contains experiences that we have repressed from awareness. Unlike Freud, he proposed that we also have access to a deep pool of knowledge, the *collective or transpersonal unconscious*. The collective unconscious contains memory traces from our ancestral past. It is psychic residue of human and animal ancestry that accumulates over many generations and propels our evolution. The collective unconscious is made up of *archetypes*: symbolic images representing universal thoughts, with corresponding strong emotions. Thus, kernels of knowing exist inside each of us in the form of archetypes. The importance of this idea is that we all have access to knowledge and deep wisdom about ourselves and life.

Two of Jung's archetypes that I find very personally and professional helpful are the *self* and the *shadow*. The self is often referred to as our internal wise person, which strives for wholeness, centeredness, and meaning, especially through the avenues associated with religion and spirituality. When connected to our self, we are connected to the wisdom of the collective unconscious and to sustainable meaning in our lives. For most of us, the first half of life is devoted to the service of the ego while the second half our strivings shift to the realization of the self. In other words, as we age we tend to become more aware of the opportunities to live in closer accordance with our soul's intentions for our life, a process described in James Hollis' book, "Finding Meaning in the Second Half of Life." Our self becomes our intuitive guide as we courageously take responsibility for our lives and for embracing what is meaningful, a concept that is central throughout this book.

The shadow archetype consists of animal instincts that humans inherited in our evolution, traits we often deem as primitive or uncivilized. The shadow is all that we would like *not* to be. It is the unconscious, compensatory side to our ego ideal, i.e., who we consciously want to be. Along with repression, projection protects our ego from the anxiety associated with recognizing our shadow and our potential to act on those needs. Projection involves attributing or seeing qualities in others that we deny in ourselves, thus keeping us safe from recognizing and owning our shadow. For example, if you are frightened by anger, it is likely that you have banished (i.e., repressed) your own anger into the shadow of your personality. When you deny your own anger, you will likely be unconsciously drawn to another person who expresses anger more easily than you do, even if it repulses you, which leads you to consciously attempt to eliminate expressions of anger in the other person. In other words, you project your denied anger onto the other person, who acts it out for you even as you try to change that person.

The importance of the shadow and corresponding inter-personal dynamics cannot be overstated, particularly when we try to embrace psychological and spiritual health, because of the tendency to over-value our ego ideal (i.e., who we think we *should* be). The more rigidly you separate your ego ideal and your shadow, the bigger your shadow becomes, increasing the likelihood that you will act out your needs in ways that you will regret. Chapter Eight will be devoted to the integration of the shadow to promote sustainable psychological and spiritual health.

Relational Models: Object Relations and Attachment Theories

Object relations consists of a loosely defined cluster of theories most represented by the thinking of Melanie Klein, W. R. D. Fairbairn, Margaret Mahler, Otto Kernberg, D. W. Winnicott, Heinz Kohut, and, more recently, James Masterson and Stephen Mitchell. Attachment theory is most associated with

John Bowlby and Mary Ainsworth. Although significant differences in concepts and language exist between object relations and attachment theories, essential aspects of the theories are remarkably similar. In particular, these theories share a focus on the processes through which our sense of self develops within the context of early parent-child interactions.

From this perspective, the process of developing a sense of self occurs through stages or developmental pathways, with the central developmental task being the dialectic between connection and separateness. Specifically, children and caregivers need to form a strong attachment bond, and yet children ultimately need to become separate psychologically. Theoretically, if children can form a strong attachment bond with parents and also feel supported in their attempts at separation and exploring the world, children develop a stable sense of self that allows them to *self-soothe* when not in contact with parents. Children can bring to mind an image of a caring, supportive parent even when they are not in physical contact with their parents. This self-soothing process allows them to develop a sense of self and to tolerate the anxiety associated with autonomy. The child's early successes with separation from and connection with parents set a trajectory for healthy development and lead to a variety of self-soothing strategies as the child grows. Strategies for self-soothing may include talking oneself through a stressful event, connecting to a core sense of identity, connecting to feelings of competency or safety, and returning to familiar and grounding activities. The ability to self-soothe in the face of anxiety is a central barometer of health throughout life.

At the core of these *relational models* are the beliefs that humans need contact with others and are psychologically formed

Rick Johnson Ph.D.

through their relationships. We are pre-wired for connecting with others, mostly for survival reasons. Relational theorists argue that a person's basic sense of self develops in a relational context. In other words, we learn who we are and what we can expect from others through repeated interactions with significant others, most notably our parents. The repeated interactions with parents, caregivers, and others (e.g., siblings) form a kind of *foundational blueprint* for a child's emerging sense of self. These blueprints have been given various names, such as self-object templates and internal relational working models.

More specifically, children learn about interpersonal issues and themes such as trust, efficacy, personal boundaries, power, and core feelings of esteem or shame through their interactions with significant others. If, for example, a child experiences repeated parental neglect during times when the child is afraid, the child may become clingy or learn to not trust others. If a child learns that she can bully her parents, the child may develop an exaggerated sense of importance and power and use bullying behaviors with others in different contexts. If a child experiences a male caregiver (i.e., father) as critical and unaccepting, the child may see subsequent men as judgmental and relate to them as if they will be critical. Thus, significant relationships early in children's lives create relational blueprints that define expectations of subsequent treatment by others and toward others.

Interestingly, these blueprints and expectations are often self-fulfilling. In other words, when we relate to someone with an expectation that we will be treated a certain way, many times it comes true. This provides one explanation for the repetition compulsion that Freud noted. Specifically, we recreate past themes and relational issues over and over through a process of choosing others who are a complementary match for our relational blueprints and then acting based on our internalized expectations. When we act toward others from a position of expecting them to treat us certain ways, we actually encourage others to live up to those expectations, a process that object relations theorists call projective identification.

One aspect of relational blueprints that is central to these theories is the balance of proximity and distance in relationships. Infants and young children need their parents' and caregivers' help and closeness to meet their basic needs and to survive. As they get older, children also have increasing awareness of their separateness from parents and others. This dual awareness of needing their parents and being separate from their parents creates a tension, and represents a universal aspect of human existence. Parents also have the same dualistic needs: to be close to their children and to have separate lives for themselves. The relational blueprint that forms when children and parents navigate these competing needs sets the stage for children's future relationships, including with their own children. This struggle between our needs for connection and separateness is a life-long condition, expressed in every relationship, especially intimate ones. Our ability to navigate these oftentimes opposing needs is a primary marker of psychological and relational health.

Interpersonal Theories: Sullivan and Horney

Harry Stack Sullivan, regarded as the grandfather of interpersonal theory and as providing an American alternative to British object relations theories, developed a theory that has been influential in contemporary communications theories and family systems theories. Similar to object relations and attachment theories, Sullivan believed that we develop internalized blueprints of ourselves in relationships, which we learn through repetitive

Rick Johnson Ph.D.

interactions with significant others. Although similar to object relations and attachment theories, Sullivan expanded these ideas and more clearly defined the role of social context and interpersonal interaction in personality development.

Sullivan argued that, although early parent-child interactions are foundational in the development of a sense of self, repetitive interactions with parents and significant others continue to affect our expectations of ourselves and others throughout childhood, adolescence, and beyond. Sullivan also extended Freud's concept of defenses and shifted the purpose of defenses into a relational context. From his viewpoint, defenses are not simply protecting the ego from anxiety created though the conflict between id and superego needs. Rather, defenses are seen as interpersonal strategies or skills that manage the anxiety generated when attachment to others is threatened. These interpersonal strategies or skills also serve the function of helping people maintain a familiar role in their relationships, often called interpersonal positions. Common interpersonal positions include: dominating others, being aloof toward others, and pleasing or caretaking others.

Sullivan also introduced the concepts of complementarity of roles and symmetrical escalation, which have been highly influential in family systems theories. Complementarity refers to the process through which interdependent behaviors tend to escalate in opposite directions. One person's behavior or communication often invites or "pulls" for a complementary response from other people (e.g., aggressive behavior tends to invite or "pull" for a response of obedience in another person). Common complementary interpersonal positions are: overfunctioner and underfunctioner, distancer and pursuer, dominant and passive, critical parent and rebellious adolescent, and stoicism and emotional expressiveness.

An example might be the more one person uses a pursuing strategy, presumably to maintain a familiar interpersonal position, the more the other person uses a distancing strategy, and vice-versa.

However, in addition to eliciting a complementary response, patterned interpersonal positions can also elicit a symmetrical response, one that is similar to the provoking position. For example, sometimes an aggressive behavior will provoke an aggressive response from others. Symmetrical and complementary interpersonal positions tend to result in our feeling out of balance, and experiencing ourselves in an increasingly restricted role vis-à-vis others.

Karen Horney provided her own version of interpersonal theory, something that has been termed psychoanalytic humanism. She introduced the concept of the Real Self, the part of us that contains our growth potentials. Although similar in some ways to Freud's original view of the ego, Horney's conception of the Real Self has more in common with Jung's self archetype. The primary motivation of the Real Self is to strive for health, meaning, and life-enhancing experiences.

The Real Self naturally emerges under relatively optimal life circumstances. With favorable parenting and life circumstances (e.g., predictable love, respect, support) a child develops feelings of belonging and security and the Real Self flourishes. Conversely, when parenting or life is characterized by unfavorable circumstances (e.g., neglect, abuse, traumatic loss, unsupportive parents) the child experiences basic anxiety (generalized feelings of insecurity, discomfort, loneliness, and helplessness) and development becomes based upon the idealized self (i.e., who we think we *should* be) rather than the Real Self. Put simply, when our life and upbringing are supportive and without trauma, our natural tendency is to strive to our potentials and flourish in our lives. The more life is characterized by unfavorable parental and environmental conditions, the more we move away from our Real Self and utilize interpersonal strategies, like those proposed by Sullivan, to cope with life circumstances and the associated basic anxiety.

Horney described three compensatory solutions or interpersonal strategies that children employ to combat basic anxiety: (a) moving toward others, (b) moving away from others, and (c) moving against others. These are also called compromise solutions, a term that highlights that these solutions, although necessary to deal with unfavorable circumstances, are clearly not as healthy for the individual as behaviors that would be chosen by the Real Self—they are compromises to make the best of the situation. Solutions initially employed by children often become patterned and are used throughout their lives. We typically employ all three solutions, but tend to have a primary solution that we use regularly, turning to other solutions if the first one is thwarted. Everyone uses some form of these solutions at different times. The more rigidly and persistently the strategies are employed, the more their use can become problematic.

The compromise solution of moving toward others involves reducing anxiety by approaching people and attempting to gain their love and approval. Over time, this can lead to the suppression of our own expansive needs and drives and the acceptance of a self-subordinating position with others. That is, we see our needs as less worthwhile than others' needs. When we use this solution as our primary interpersonal strategy we develop a very low sense of personal entitlement and trade in our own achievement needs for the love of another. As an example, personal needs for education or career may become ignored or overshadowed by our partner's achievement plans. We often find intimate partners that will take care of us and, at worst, control us by threatening love withdrawal. When severely out-of-balance, we become increasingly dependent on others, move further away from our own personal power, and run the risk of being emotionally and physically abused by a partner.

The compromise solution of moving away from others involves reducing anxiety by avoiding contact with others and their perceived demands. When we use this as our primary solution we detach from life and often exhibit an absence of striving and an aversion to effort, goal-direction, and planning. We tend to restrict our own expansive needs and wishes and are hypersensitive and reactive to perceived influence and coercion from others. We tend to be unemployed or self-employed because we have difficulty working for others. Horney described three subtypes in this group: (a) those that are persistently resigned to live a restricted life, (b) those that are rebellious and reactive to authority and the demands of others, and (c) those that focus on fun and avoidance of hard work.

The compromise solution of moving against others involves reducing anxiety by attempting to control or master life's circumstances. Strategies associated with this solution tend to include engaging in achievement activities and maintaining extremely high standards of oneself and others. Although these are not inherently problematic qualities, as with all the solutions they become problematic when out-of-balance and motivated by fear. When we use this as our primary solution we tend to overwork and achieve based on underlying feelings of inadequacy and fears of being discovered as incompetent. In other words, we achieve based on fear and overcompensation rather than joy. Horney described three subtypes associated with extreme forms of this solution: (a) narcissism: those that need constant confirmation of their talents and admiration of others, (b) perfectionism: those that adopt exceedingly high standards for themselves and others and tend to strive to control as many aspects of their life as they can, and (c) arrogant vindictiveness: those that are exceedingly competitive, need to triumph over others, and are prone to violent rages.

Humanism: Rogers

In stark contrast to the Freudian view that humans are driven primarily by instinctual impulses within the id, that unconscious thoughts and feelings have a dramatic impact on a person's actions, and that the human personality is largely formed during the first six years of life, Carl Rogers proposed that humans are innately positive and have free will that can be expressed across the life-span. Rogers's approach, termed person-centered therapy, focused on facilitating a person's inner potentials and ownership of options and choices. He believed each person has inner dignity and unique value and possesses the ability to know what is life-affirming and life-enhancing. At our core, we have *inner wisdom* and *inner knowing* about what is positive for us in our lives.

Along with other humanistic theorists, Rogers argued that if basic needs are met (e.g., food, shelter, safety, and love), we have a natural tendency to strive for self-actualization. Self-actualization refers to the process of embracing one's potentials and transcending limitations that are self-imposed or internalized. Self-actualization can be expressed and experienced through a variety of creative and unique ways and is individually defined. For some of us, self-actualization is experienced through accomplishments or peak experiences. For others, it is experienced through everyday activities. The central and defining aspect of actualization experiences is that they contribute to our growth and potentials in life-enhancing ways.

Rogers also believed we have a learned sense of self, which is based on the perception of regard by others (i.e., what others, especially our parents, think of us). Under relatively optimal parenting and life circumstances, we will make life-enhancing choices and will de-value experiences that are contrary to the self-actualization process. In other words, if parents and significant others had positive life-affirming views of us as children, we internalize their positive regard and strive to actualize our potentials. Conversely, if parenting and life circumstances are characterized by abuse and life-detracting experiences, we internalize those experiences and oftentimes move away from our unique potentials and lose touch with our inner knowing.

As we age and become adults, we have more and more freedom to make choices in our lives. Sometimes these choices can involve difficult decisions related to listening to our own inner wisdom versus allowing others to dictate to us what they think is good for us. Rogers did not advocate rejecting others' advice per se. He simply believed if we can quiet down and focus our awareness on our own internal wisdom, we will find our own answers and know what is right for us. Unfortunately, many of us, due to fear of not being loved or accepted by others, stop listening to our innate inner wisdom. This *de-selfing* process, which will be expanded upon in Chapter Four, is one of the primary ways we lose touch with our Real Self and suffer in our lives.

Rogers' immense contributions to the field of psychology focus on his unwavering belief that within all of us exists an *inner wise person* that can guide and direct us in our lives. He believed it is disrespectful to assume what is best for others or to tell them what to do with their lives. Rather, he urged therapists to turn clients inward to reconnect with their own inner knowing and develop clarity in their needs and choices. Then, clients are encouraged to act courageously in accordance with this wisdom, even if it means disappointing others. Generally speaking, it's better to love yourself and take ownership for your decisions than to allow others to define or control you. Rogers' approach can be uncomfortable at times to fully embrace. However, once you start to truly grasp the notion that the wisdom and clarity you seek already exists within you, you can experience the exhilaration of your freedom as well as ownership of your personal power.

Family Systems Theories: Minuchin and Bowen

Salvador Minuchin, originally trained as a psychoanalyst, broke from individually-oriented paradigms to develop a theory that considers individuals' behavior within their cultural and familial contexts. His approach, called structural family therapy, provides a model for conceptualizing how the organization of a family influences the psychological health of each of its members. Family structure is the organizational glue that provides the transactional rules of each family system, the operating rules. Certain family structures support the growth of members while other structures inhibit it.

Each of us is born into a nuclear family with its own set of rules, roles and belief systems. Rules are expectations for certain types of behaviors. Examples include expectations of a spouse, children, and extended family as well as rules for how conflict is resolved and how emotions and intimacy are expressed. Roles are based on a predictable set of expected behaviors for individual family members that become patterned over time, such as being the quiet one, the shy one, or the responsible one. Belief systems are ideas about the world or family life that become shared realities for family members. Examples include shared beliefs about religion, gender roles, definitions of success and achievement, and the definition of family. Healthy rules, roles, and beliefs support the family structure while at the same time allow family members to grow and meet their individual needs. Conversely, dysfunctional families lack sustainable structures and inhibit the attainment of developmentally-appropriate needs of individuals.

Minuchin popularized the term, *boundaries*, which is a key marker of family structure. Boundaries regulate the amount and type of affiliation and information that flow between people or groups. Rigid boundaries allow for little affiliation between people and lead to disengaged relationships, which are characterized by emotional distance and lack of intimacy. Diffuse boundaries permit a great deal of affiliation between people and lead to enmeshed relationships, which are characterized by too much connection and a lack of separateness and autonomy. Healthy boundaries exist in the middle ground between the extremes of enmeshment and disengagement and provide a balance of connection and separation in family relationships.

Along with boundaries, families can be conceptualized as consisting of *subsystems*: such as parental, spousal, sibling, etc. Each subsystem has its own functions. The parental subsystem is the executive branch of the family and arguably the most important for healthy family functioning. When the parental subsystem is operating effectively by providing appropriate levels of love, limits, and guidance, children typically progress well in their lives and have opportunities to reach their potentials. When this executive subsystem is not operating well (e.g., not enough love, inconsistent or unreasonable limits, or lack of developmentally-appropriate guidance and mentoring), structural problems ensue that threaten the ability of members to develop normally. Additional problematic structures and their corresponding difficulties for individual development will be discussed in Chapter Four.

Family systems theory, also called *transgenerational theory* to clarify it as different from communication-based family systems models, was developed by Murray Bowen. Transgenerational theory focuses on how our sense of self develops in the context of emotional attachments in our multigenerational family system. While Minuchin focuses on current family dynamics, Bowen highlights how rules, roles and belief systems are passed down from generation to generation, a dynamic he termed the *multigenerational transmission process.*

When children grow up and start their own nuclear families, the partners negotiate (albeit largely unconsciously) to determine the rules of engagement of their new family. I call this developmental phase of coupleship, "Whose Reality Wins," because newly married or committed couples often argue about whose family of origin relational rules will predominate. This negotiation process is what is often addressed and made more explicit in pre-marital counseling.

The central concept of family systems theory is *differentiation of self*, a multi-faceted concept that will be expanded upon in greater detail in Chapters Four and Six. Differentiation is narrowly defined as the ability of a family member to be separate and autonomous while remaining in contact with other family members. In other words, an individual with a high level of differentiation has a separate sense of self, yet doesn't cut off contact to achieve this separateness. This balance of separateness and connection, which is termed *emotional middle ground*, is a primary predictor of psychological health in adults.

The process of differentiating from our family of origin is seen as the primary developmental task of young adulthood. This process requires us to challenge what we have been taught in our families and come to a place of personal ownership of identity issues such as religious, political, and philosophical ideologies, lifestyle, career, and relationships. True ownership of our identity requires neither blindly accepting all that has been taught by our family and significant adults nor reactively rejecting what has been taught.

Bowen argued that we are often only as differentiated as our parents, and tend to find intimate partners with similar differentiation levels. Our differentiation levels are then passed down to our children; and the cycle continues.

Control-Mastery Theory: Weiss

Control-mastery theory was originated and developed by Joseph Weiss, with the theory's tenets being researched and tested by Weiss, Harold Sampson, and others at the San Francisco Psychotherapy Research Group (formerly the Mount Zion Psychotherapy Research Group). Control-mastery theory is a contemporary, integrative theory that has been termed a cognitive-psychoanalytic theory because it integrates cognitive theory into an extension of Freud's later ideas. The result is a wonderfully rich and useful theory of personality and psychotherapy approach.

Weiss extends Freud's later writings by proposing that the ego is not simply managing anxiety generated through the internal conflict between the selfish demands of the id and moralistic demands of the superego. Weiss argues that the ego has it's own energy, which is focused on adapting to the environment, making sense of life events, and maintaining connection with parents. For survival purposes, children have a need to stay connected to their parents and have an innate ability and drive to make sense of the events and interactions that occur throughout their lives. The idea is that we are constantly categorizing and defining our worlds. Simply stated, we are meaning makers. Traumatic and emotionally unsettling experiences, especially those that threaten attachment to parents (e.g., abuse, neglect, abandonment), create a strong urgency to make sense of these experiences. If we can understand why events happen, then we can possibly avoid the traumatic experiences in the future.

The following diagram helps illustrate the central tenets of this theory.

Experiences----Emotions/Feelings----Thoughts/Beliefs----Behaviors

Both repetitive and nodal experiences, especially traumatic ones, create emotional responses within us. The more traumatic and uncomfortable the feelings, the more urgently we need to understand the experiences and emotions. So, when painful and difficult circumstances occur, children attempt to make sense of these events. These interpretations of events and feelings then lead to behaviors and perceived behavioral options.

Unfortunately, children tend to blame themselves when traumatic events happen to them. This occurs for several reasons. First, sometimes children are told that they are the cause of their pain. For example, after physically abusing a child a parent might say, "You deserved it because you were a bad girl." Second, because children need their parents for survival purposes, they are pre-wired to believe that their parents are willing and able to take care of them. Thus, children think that their parents wouldn't knowingly hurt them or allow them to be hurt. Third, children tend to exhibit egocentric thinking (i.e., believing that they are the center of the universe) and tend to blame themselves for what happens in their lives. The end result is their beliefs about why traumatic experiences have occurred tend to be self-blaming and "pathogenic." *Pathogenic beliefs*, acquired as the child infers causality about traumatic events, are convictions about how one must behave in order to avoid being re-traumatized. The thinking goes like this, "If I'm to blame, then I can change my behavior so I won't be hurt again." Pathogenic beliefs set parameters around what is allowable and lead to inflexible behaviors.

For example, let's say a little girl grows up with an alcoholic father who occasionally becomes angry and violent toward her and her mother. As the child watches her father's violent and unpredictable behavior, she will likely experience anxiety, fear, and confusion, and a corresponding need to understand why this is happening. Typically she may believe "Daddy drinks when he is stressed. If I can be a good girl and don't add to his stress then maybe he won't drink. If I can make him happy maybe he won't hit mommy." These pathogenic beliefs will likely lead to inflexible behaviors that are attempts to regain some control and safety in her life. For example, the child may develop inflexible behaviors focused on hyper-vigilance, caretaking, perfectionism, and removal of her own needs. She will likely develop an exaggerated sense of her personal responsibility in regards to others' behavior.

Pathogenic beliefs and associated inflexible behaviors tend to be overgeneralized to all areas of our life, and tend to stick with us throughout our lives. These inflexible behaviors also tend to be self-fulfilling. Specifically, if we approach relationships with a rigid style of caretaking and taking too much responsibility for others' lives, we tend to attract complementary types (i.e., underfunctioners) and elicit complementary behaviors from others, which reinforces our pathogenic beliefs and our perceived need for the inflexible behaviors. Thus, we get what we expect.

At the core of control-mastery theory is the belief that we want to heal past wounds, disconfirm pathogenic beliefs, and increase behavioral flexibility, although we are not always consciously aware of the ways we need to heal and the ways we are attempting to do so. Weiss argues that the ego has *unconscious plans* to disconfirm pathogenic beliefs and grow. We attempt to disconfirm pathogenic beliefs by re-enacting childhood trauma in current relationships in hopes that better outcomes will result. This tends to emerge in two ways: (a) transference tests and (b) turning passive into active. Transference tests occur when we re-enact the same old dynamic and assume the same interpersonal position (e.g., caretaker, responsible one, etc.) as when the pathogenic beliefs first started to form during childhood. Turning passive into active occurs when we re-enact the same old dynamic and adopt the other person's interpersonal position (e.g., dad's drunken irresponsibility) and find someone who will play our childhood role (e.g., responsible one). Either way, we hope the outcome will be different and we will resolve the trauma and disconfirm the pathogenic beliefs.

In our previous example, the girl may enact a transference test by choosing intimate partners who are alcoholic, violent, or unpredictable in hopes of finding a solution to her original experiences with her father. Thus, control-mastery theory provides a growth-oriented explanation for the repetition compulsion that Freud noted. That is, we are not simply repeating what we witnessed or experienced as children; rather, we are drawn to similar relationships again and again in hopes of healing unresolved trauma and disconfirming pathogenic beliefs. Unfortunately, these attempts are often re-traumatizing and end up reinforcing pathogenic beliefs (e.g., "All men are irresponsible and it's my job to take care of them.").

From a control-mastery perspective, we are trying to heal and unconsciously know what we need. We are often limited, however, in our awareness of our options of how to heal. In this approach, psychotherapists see their clients as co-therapists in the process and as experts on themselves and what they need. A therapist's job is to help clients become aware of their unresolved traumas and associated pathogenic beliefs, inflexible behaviors, and unconscious plans to heal and grow. Therapists help make unconscious plans conscious, and then support clients as they make behavioral changes in accordance with their plans.

Internal Family Systems: Schwartz

Internal Family Systems (IFS) is a contemporary theory, which was developed by Richard Schwartz as an integration of family systems models, Jungian theory, and various theorists who propose that our personality is comprised of parts. The resulting integrative theory is an empowering and non-pathologizing view of human functioning and an approach to healing and growth.

Schwartz describes parts within people as subpersonalities that interact with each other and the outside world. The parts have healthy preferred roles, which can become extreme and problematic, mostly due to traumatic life experiences. Schwartz divides the personality into four major parts: (a) self, (b) managers, (c) exiles, and (d) firefighters.

The self, borrowed from Jung's self archetype, is the core of the personality. The self is the part of us that seeks meaning and integration in our lives. When we are balanced, the self acts as a wise leader and exhibits characteristics such as calmness, curiosity, compassion, confidence, creativity, connectedness, courage, and clarity. Everyone has a self. However, extreme behaviors from the other parts can limit the self from assuming an active and compassionate leadership role within the personality. Sometimes, the other parts have been leading for so long they do not trust that the self will lead effectively. In situations where people have endured trauma and abuse, they lose touch with their self and tend to define their personalities as consisting solely of the other parts. In other words, they have very limited ability to connect with or access the characteristics of the self.

Managers run the day-to-day aspects of most people's lives. They attempt to keep us safe and functional by maintaining control of our world. These are the very responsible parts that remind us to follow the rules, keep our jobs, be on time for appointments, and stay in control in relationships. Managers play roles such as controller, striver, caretaker, pleaser, judge, critic, passive pessimist, and planner. When they are in-balance, managers help us function in our lives. When out-of-balance, they urge us to make fear-based decisions designed to avoid change and eliminate risk. The fear is that if control is lost, bad things will happen.

Exiles are those parts of the personality that hold painful, raw emotions and experiences. They are the vulnerable parts that have experienced pain and trauma, and tend to be isolated from the rest of the internal system. They become extreme when they are not being heard or validated by the other parts, which happens periodically because the other parts avoid the raw and scary emotions contained in the exiles. Any emotions that are deemed unacceptable can be exiled by the other parts, which is similar to Jung's idea of the shadow archetype. Typical examples are shame, fear, neediness, loneliness, anger, grief, abandonment, and any memories associated with childhood trauma (e.g., verbal, physical, sexual abuse).

Firefighters are the parts that jump to action whenever an exiled part floods us with painful emotions, memories, or sensations that overwhelm the managers' abilities to control the situation. Firefighters act to repress the emerging exiles and distract us by impulsively seeking stimulation that can override the pain. Examples of firefighting behaviors include addictive behaviors (drugs, alcohol, food, sex, work, shopping, gambling, etc.), rage, violence, self-mutilation, suicidal thoughts and behaviors, and dissociation.

Many of us spend the majority of our conscious lives moving between managers, exiles, and firefighters and have lost significant contact with the self. Most people define who they are almost exclusively from the manager sense of consciousness. The main goal of IFS is to return the self to its rightful leadership role of the internal system, which includes supporting the other parts in finding their voice and assuming healthy roles. In other words, all parts need to be heard, but the self needs to run the show.

Thematic Integration of Theories

Although the various models presented in this chapter are quite different, several themes emerge from these theories. First, there is convergence around the idea that structures exist within the personality, with the core essence of the personality being some form of inner wisdom and intuitive knowing. Whether we are talking about ego, the self or the Real Self, a number of these theories propose that on some level we know what is good for us and what will be affirming in our lives. In this book I refer to this inner wisdom and core sense of ourselves as the Real Self, the part of us that contains the collective knowledge described by Jung and wants to heal from traumatic and unresolved experiences, to grow and actualize our potentials, and to provide compassionate leadership in our lives.

These theories also repeatedly point to the importance of relationships. Our basic sense of who we are is formed in the context of relationships, especially our families. In our families we learn about personal boundaries, roles, relational rules, parenting, and myriad other relational themes, such as intimacy, conflict, trust, and the dialectic between separateness and relatedness. The types of interactions we have throughout childhood and beyond have a great influence on how we think and feel about ourselves and others, how we expect to be treated by others, and the behavioral options and intimate relationships we choose. And, most important, relationships provide the primary vehicle for healing, growth, joy, and abundance.

To some extent, all of these theories focus on the role of anxiety in personality formation and our ability to live a happy and successful life. Anxiety is a natural part of living. A primary source of anxiety comes from actual or perceived threats to significant relationships, first and foremost with parents. A certain amount of anxiety can be beneficial in that it can motivate us to tackle difficult tasks and to connect with our own strengths, autonomy, and competency. However, too much anxiety can be overwhelming. Thus, everyone needs to find ways to manage anxiety and learn to self-soothe, with the use of intrapsychic and interpersonal defenses or strategies being inevitable and necessary in this process. What matters most are the types of strategies we employ, the degree of rigidity vs. flexibility in these strategies, and the degree to which our strategies are motivated by fear vs. health.

These theories also describe typical difficulties for people, with the most problematic occurring when traumatic or repetitive experiences produce overwhelming anxiety. Based on inferences about traumatic experiences, pathogenic beliefs about ourselves and the world are developed and often lead to inflexible behaviors. Thus, in an attempt to make sense of and manage the anxiety associated with trauma and threats to primary relationships, we move away from the actualizing tendencies of the Real Self and utilize compromise solutions, which tend to be self fulfilling. That is, when we employ strategies to protect ourselves, we often end up receiving confirmation of our fears and get what we expect from others in relationships.

Different theories have various explanations for why we seem to repeat painful experiences and relationships over and over. Weiss' theory, in addition to conceptualizing this as a repetition of familiar relational blueprints, provides a growth-oriented explanation that assumes we repeat experiences in an attempt to gain control and mastery over unresolved and traumatic experiences. Once again, the idea is we have inner wisdom and a drive to heal and grow.

Jung, Horney, Rogers, and Schwartz specifically point to the existence of creative and transcendent energy within all of us. Jung, in particular, emphasized the role of spirituality in health and healing. Building on the foundation of these ideas, the central tenet of this book is that human health is greatly enhanced by an integration of psychological and spiritual practice. When the Real Self is aligned with and embraces spirituality, we have the capacity to experience guiding and healing energy as well as clarity, creativity, meaning, and sustainable abundance in our lives. In the next chapter, I will discuss various ways of understanding, experiencing, and accessing spirituality.

Chapter 3
Spirituality

Face of God

    I wept
    uncontrolled
    as my open mouth
    breath
    reached its full
    expanse.
    Shuddering
    each time
    my lungs filled,
    trying not to think,
    my face aching
    as I let
    myself cry
    and be no more
    than present
    to the crying.

    Afterwards I sat
    in the streaming
    energy.
    I sat
    in gratitude
    and wonder.
    Breathing

Rick Johnson Ph.D.

> the soft scent
> of desert sage,
> breathing
> the scorching sun,
> breathing
> the red sandstone mesas,
> breathing
> each atom
> of blue sky,
> breathing
> in and out
> the sweet taste
> of peace.
>
> Anson Wright, *Sandstone Monastery*[1]

"I get glimpses." I have heard many people say this phrase when talking about spirituality. I have said it many times too. What does this phrase mean? Glimpses of what? What do we "see?" How do we know it is there? What is the "Face of God?"

As part of my own search to find answers to these questions, I have asked countless numbers of people three questions:

- What is your personal definition of spirituality?
- How have you experienced spirituality in your life?
- How do you access or practice your spirituality?

What I found is that spirituality is uniquely defined and experienced, yet common themes emerge. These themes provide a foundation to discuss the very personal topic of spirituality in broad and inclusive ways.

People of faith often answer questions about their spirituality with certainty and with language that is true to their faith structures. Many people believe that their way of knowing spirituality is the only "right" way. For some, spirituality is based on a relationship with an active and intentional force or entity that is external to them. For others, the experience of spirituality is internal. Others experience an external sense of spirituality that is not intentional (e.g., nature). Still others view spirituality as synonymous with religion and religious doctrine, while many others separate spirituality from organized religion.

Along with a multitude of ways of conceptualizing spirituality, people use various names to express personal and paradigm-based definitions of spirituality. Although far from an exhaustive list, some of the names for or ways of understanding spirituality that many people use include:

- God (as defined by different religious faiths)
- Holy Spirit
- Spirit
- Soul
- Essence
- Higher Self
- Source
- Transcendence
- Divine
- Love
- Joy
- Purity
- Oneness
- Interconnectedness
- Interbeing
- Energy-between-things
- Light
- Clarity
- Potentialities

Rick Johnson Ph.D.

- Flow
- Nature and natural beauty
- Creative and artistic expression
- Vision
- Guiding Force
- Life Force
- Life Energy

Other people describe physical sensations and sensory perceptions they associate with spirituality. Just a few of the many sensations I have personally experienced or heard others describe are:

- feeling like a comforting presence is near or enveloping them
- sensations of being held or comforted
- a deep knowing in their chest or stomach
- a knowing that they are not alone
- feeling like they are deeply cared for by a larger force
- "tingly" and warm feelings on their body or skin
- a warm light or sensations entering their body, head, or heart
- spontaneous relief from emotional or physical suffering
- feelings of peace and clarity
- experiencing coincidences and connections
- a sense of being part of something larger
- feelings of being interconnected with all things
- "seeing" or sensing energy fields
- moments of clarity and perspective on time and space
- "seeing" or feeling glimpses of truths in the world or in one's sense of being

It is easy to offend or alienate people when talking about spirituality. If the "wrong" words are used, people often turn away from the message; they believe the words don't represent their relationship with or understanding of spirituality. Simply put, spirituality is a very personal issue.

Although I don't remember the exact event, I have been told by my mother that when I was a 5 year old boy, I was asked by my devoutly religious grandmother if I believed in God. I supposedly said, "God is a chemical." My grandmother nearly fainted! I don't know why I said this. It's possible, I suppose, that I had glimpses into the nature of spirituality. Maybe I was repeating what I heard from someone else. Or, maybe I simply wanted to tease my grandmother. Whatever the reason I said it, it seems as though I was already on a path trying to form my own personal understanding of and relationship with spirituality.

I have come to a place in my life where the specific name people use to label spirituality doesn't matter much to me. I have my own faith structure, which tends to be broad and inclusive. I think we are all trying to understand and talk about the same thing. Huston Smith, a renowned religious scholar, describes spirituality as a prize that sits atop a large pyramid, with many paths heading up the pyramid to reach the prize. Some people prefer to ride around the base of the pyramid trying to get converts to join them on their wagons. Unfortunately, they can spend all of their time and energy riding around the base rather than moving up the pyramid and developing their own personal relationship with spirituality.

It is my intention to discuss spirituality in ways that encourage readers to generate and work within their own views and personal definitions of spirituality. For the purpose of writing this book, however, I felt compelled to provide a name for spirituality that will provide a short-hand throughout the book. It was a difficult task. Words do not capture the totality of experience with or understanding of spirituality. Any words I use run the risk of alienating others. After much thought and reflection, I chose the phrase *Spiritual Energy* to represent what I mean by spirituality. I like the phrase because it implies an active force that can be defined through various faith structures and can be personally known and embraced. I believe we all can tap into Spiritual Energy in the many forms of its manifestation, or our own particularly favored one.

Based on my intention to discuss an accessible and inclusive view of spirituality, the remainder of this chapter will focus on integrative themes that cut across many ways of knowing and relating to Spiritual Energy. These themes emerged largely from interviews with people asking about their definitions, experiences and ways of accessing spirituality in their lives. Because I am most familiar with Christian and Buddhist perspectives, examples and supporting citations will mostly be from these two faith traditions. I will not attempt to summarize the many different faith traditions, to provide an in-depth comparison of different faiths, or to provide a comprehensive discussion of any particular perspective on spirituality. Rather, the purpose of the chapter is to discuss key themes that are relevant across faith traditions and are useful for integrating with psychological approaches to growth and healing. As Brother Wayne Teasdale writes in his book, "The Mystic Heart," when spiritual traditions meet, greater truths can be realized.

Remembering

How often do you experience clarity about what is truly right for you in your life? Do you sense an inner voice or external wisdom which tries to remind you of who you are? Do you periodically have glimpses of larger truths? Do these moments of clarity and perspective feel confirmatory of what you already know on an intuitive level?

The first theme I want to discuss is the heart-felt sense many people have that they already possess spiritual knowledge. When people experience spiritual insights, they often describe the feeling as being confirmatory, as though they are remembering something rather than learning it for the first time. Many describe it as a feeling of "already knowing," or at least having glimpses of knowing. For most, this feeling of knowing is hard to put into words. It occurs on an intuitive level and can emerge through many different avenues, such as looking deeply at a sunset or a piece of art, listening deeply to the sounds of a stream rippling over rocks, and opening one's heart during prayer and spiritual reflection. The remembering inevitably brings perspective and clarity on their lives as well as feelings of certitude, calmness, joy, and solidity.

Inner Knowing and External Presence

How does spirituality emerge in your consciousness? Do you sense an inner voice of spiritual wisdom? Does your experience of spiritual knowledge come to you from sources outside yourself?

The sense of remembering spiritual wisdom and knowing seems to come from both internal and external sources and is described by many faiths. One way to understand external spiritual presence is reflected in the Christian view of the Holy Spirit, which is understood generally as the energy sent by God. Brother David Steindl-Rast defines the Holy Spirit as the breath of divine life and argues that, "From a biblical perspective, there has never been a human being that is not alive with God's own life breath." Many people describe the feeling that the Holy Spirit (Spiritual Energy) has always been available to them, even when they have chosen to not access it or have had only a faint sense of its presence. It's a feeling or sense that Spiritual Energy is waiting to be invited into our lives. This experience is exemplified by comments a client recently made to me, "Even when I turned my back on God, I knew he was there waiting for me. I always felt his presence, even though I wasn't ready to accept him into my life." Along with prayer and reflective practice, external presence is often known and experienced through both transcendent and ordinary experiences, including relationships with others, beholding nature and natural beauty, and creative and artistic expression. Thus, an aspect of spirituality seems to be a feeling of remembering what we already know and remembering to connect with the Spiritual Energy that is available to us.

Inner knowing of Spiritual Energy is described by those from many different faiths. From a Christian perspective, connecting to inner knowing is often equated with connecting with the Holy Spirit within us. "We know that we live in him and he in us, because he has given us of his Spirit."[2]

Buddhists provide other ways of understanding this sense of inner knowing, including reincarnation and the belief that we all possess *Buddha nature*. Buddha nature is the seed of enlightenment and spiritual knowledge that exists in every person. Buddha nature represents our potential to become fully awake.

From these perspectives, we all possess the potential for knowing deep truths. One primary goal of spiritual practice, therefore, is to unleash and facilitate our access to the knowledge that already exists within us.

In his immensely powerful and inclusive book, "Living

Buddha, Living Christ," Thich Nhat Hanh, a prominent Vietnamese Buddhist monk and teacher, provides a beautiful integration of not only Buddhism and Christianity, but of the concepts of Buddha nature and the Holy Spirit. He argues that when we live our lives being aware of and awake in the present moment, we activate our inner potential and connect with the Holy Spirit. Thereby, we invite the Holy Spirit into our hearts and lives. Every moment offers opportunities to be awake to the Spiritual Energy existing within and around us.

This spiritual integration mirrors the integration I am proposing in this book. Specifically, I believe each of us has access to Spiritual Energy both through inner knowing and connection to external presence. When we embrace our Real Self, we touch "God's own life breath." This connection to the Real Self provides a conduit to the Spiritual Energy that exists within and around us. When the inner knowing of the Real Self meets the Spiritual Energy of external presence, we develop the capacity for sustained joy and abundance in our lives.

Transcendent and Ordinary Experiences

Where do you find and experience the divine? Is it available to you most readily through intense, mind-shifting experiences? Does it emerge in the routines and experiences of everyday life?

While sitting atop a mountain or hilltop with a view of the surrounding environment, it's easy for many of us to embrace the majesty and profound beauty of our world. During periods of intense prayer and spiritual practice, people can experience intense bodily and emotional sensations. Peak experiences, such as these two examples, tend to interrupt our perceptions of everyday experience of life and provide us with glimpses of a transcendent perspective. During moments of transcendence, some people report having visions of being part of an intricate interconnected web of life, being connected to God or Spiritual Energy, or having glimpses into the nature of reality, to name a few reactions. The point is that entering into peak or transcendent experiences allows us to have insights and perspectives that we don't normally have in day-to-day living.

In addition to transcendent experiences, many people report having spiritual experiences throughout their everyday lives. Whether we are looking at a tree while walking during a lunch hour, compassionately seeing the beauty and suffering in another person's face, or simply washing the dishes after dinner, each moment contains possibilities for us to see deeply into the nature of life. This idea can be seen in a famous Buddhist saying: "Before enlightenment the Monk chops wood and carries water. After enlightenment the Monk chops wood and carries water." After enlightenment, the Monk does the same chores; however, the Monk's experience of his chores is different. He is more awake to the present moment and to the experience of the chore. Each moment contains all of life.

In his book, "Ordinary Mind," Barry Magid describes the ideas of transcendent and everyday spiritual practices as "Top down" and "Bottom up." Top down spiritual practice is intended to induce a peak experience, usually through focused concentration that eventually brings flashes of insight and understanding. Bottom up practice, on the other hand, supports spiritual growth by being in the moment and becoming attuned to emotional and physical sensations that naturally occur as an aspect of being. An important theme, therefore, is that spirituality can be accessed through ordinary as well as exceptional experiences. The key is to be open and awake to both forms.

Present Moment Awareness

Do you find yourself consumed with and distracted by your thoughts? Does time often pass without your conscious awareness? When are you able to be fully awake in your life? Do you experience spirituality when you are aware in the present moment?

Many people report that spirituality is most accessible to them when they are awake in the present moment. Unfortunately, people typically spend the majority of their conscious awareness focused on experiences that have already occurred or on those they are anticipating. So much suffering is caused by our continual addiction to thinking about how life *should have been* or how it *needs to be* for us to be happy. "If only this hadn't happened, then I could be happy. If only this would change, then I could be happy. If only I had this relationship, then I could be happy." This isn't to say that life isn't hard. However, most of the time we create more misery by making happiness contingent upon certain conditions being met, which may be largely out of our control. And when the conditions we deemed necessary for our happiness are met, we painfully realize that the conditions are transitory. We cannot hold onto and possess the conditions. So, we feel pain and then scurry into a search for the new conditions we hope will create and support our happiness. This is a very unwise and painful cycle.

When not endlessly focusing on the past or future, many people are simply not awake: they are sleepwalking through life. They are mindlessly following ritual and routine, not aware of what is occurring within them and not intentionally engaged in their life. They often suffer from chronic feelings of boredom and alienation.

It has taken me a long time to begin to understand the

meaning and power of present moment awareness, and I'm still learning and remembering everyday. One of my first conscious lessons occurred almost 20 years ago when I was on a camping road trip across the country with a friend. We had run into some minor struggles, including several days of rain and I was feeling grumpy and started to complain. We were sitting in the tent and he said, "How are you in this present moment only?" I had to admit that I was OK, maybe even happy. I realized if I could let go of my infatuation with what had happened and what needed to happen, I was aware of an underlying happiness in the present moment. I tested it throughout the rest of our trip. Most of the time, my suffering was based on thinking about what had happened and what needed to happen. Even when I was experiencing struggles, present moment awareness seemed to bring comfort and perspective.

Years of attempting to live an aware and intentional life have only strengthened my belief in the power of present moment awareness. The present moment is where life is always lived. Even when we are reminiscing about the past, we can do so with awareness of our present experience. The present moment is where our breath is in our consciousness, where our mind can calm down, where we can be aware of our heart, and where we connect to our Real Self. Spiritual Energy is in the present moment, every moment.

Interconnectedness

How do you experience yourself in relation to others and the world? Do you feel isolated and alienated in your life? Do you feel combative against others and your environment? Do you sense that you are part of a larger whole?

I recently went to a talk by Mark Epstein, a psychiatrist

who focuses on integrating psychoanalysis and Buddhism. After his talk and as he was leaving to read his new book at a local bookstore, I asked him the same question I ask many people, "What is your definition of spirituality?" He said, "Spirituality is anything that helps us realize we are not separate selves, anything that allows us to see we are interconnected with everything else."

From Taoist and Buddhist perspectives, spirituality can be experienced through moments of knowing or experiencing oneness. We are all part of the larger whole. Voices from various fields of study, such as quantum physics, systems science, psychology, communications science, and ecology, are joining and supporting the Eastern philosophical view that all of life is interconnected by dynamic patterns of energy. Thich Nhat Hanh describes this idea as "interbeing—the Buddhist teaching that nothing can be by itself alone, that everything in the cosmos must 'interbe' with everything else."[3] As Joan Halifax says, "Buddhist practice and my study of shamanism have helped me see that we are one node in a vast web of life. As such, we are connected to each thing, and all things abide in us."[4]

Although mostly associated with Buddhism and various Eastern faith traditions, oneness can also be understood from a Christian perspective. Christians would likely describe the energy between all things as again being the Holy Spirit. "For the Spirit of the Lord fills the whole universe and holds all things together..."[5]

For many people, once they begin to grasp the ideas of oneness and interconnectedness, they no longer feel so isolated and alone in the world. They also tend to develop a deeper sense of compassion and responsibility for all beings. They begin to realize that what each of us does matters and affects everyone

Rick Johnson Ph.D.

and everything else, like energy rippling out and eventually interacting and touching all of life. They feel a sense of harmony in their lives rather than alienation and competition. As Catherine Ingram says in her book, Passionate Presence, "The deepest contentment comes from recognizing the pervading life force in everything."

Love and Fear

Do you believe life is dangerous and that people will take advantage of or hurt you if you are not vigilant? How often do you have a loving, compassionate view of yourself and others? On what do you base most of your conscious decisions and actions: fear and avoidance of what frightens you or love and generousness of spirit?

What role, if any, does fear have in healthy living? In short, the answer is that fear should have a very limited role. Fear can be a gift that informs us when something is not right. We have a natural, built-in tendency to fear things that can harm us. At its best, fear motivates us to act decisively to protect ourselves and restore safety by triggering a fight or flight response. In fact, problems can occur when we don't listen to our intuition about fear, when we ignore the signs that something is not right.

Unfortunately, after the danger is gone, fear turns from a gift into an obstacle. Fear can overwhelm and paralyze us. And, fear-based living encourages us to consistently overestimate the dangers in our world and rob us of spontaneity, joy, and generousness. Thus, although fear can serve the purpose of alerting us to danger, it more often leads to a perception that life is more dangerous than it actually is and fosters limitations in our lives. In other words, fear can inform us under limited circumstances, but should not run our lives.

Although some religions propagate fear as a means to control and direct their followers, many different faiths espouse the idea that Spiritual Energy is a loving energy. In fact, many people report that love is the central aspect of their definition of and experience with spirituality. Marianne Williamson's book, "A Return to Love: Reflections on A Course in Miracles," introduced many to the belief that fear, rather than hate, is the opposite of love. Christians generally believe that, "God is love. Whoever lives in love lives in God, and God in him. There is no fear in love. But perfect love drives out fear..."[6] Speaking from a Taoist perspective about the "Way of Love" in her book, "The Tao of Inner Peace," Diane Dreher writes, "Compassion for ourselves and others breaks down illusions of separation, bringing greater harmony to our world." The unifying idea is that embracing a loving and compassionate heart allows us to make decisions based on joy and abundance instead of fear and scarcity.

Potentialities and Free Will

To what degree do you have the ability to choose and direct your life? To what degree do forces outside yourself determine the course of your life? Do you believe your thoughts and actions define your reality and therefore have the ability to change and direct your life? Do you believe that conditions of the past and present largely determine your fate?

The interplay between free will and determination is one of the most hotly contested and controversial topics in various fields of study, including religion, psychology, physics, and philosophy. Some, including many I interviewed, place almost limitless faith in each individual's ability to create his or her own reality while others argue that life is largely predetermined. Although varying and competing points of view exist, some convergence of ideas is possible.

First, there seems to be an interaction between free will

and a larger purpose or possibilities. We seem to have some degree of free will to choose our paths in life and to determine our realities. A central tenet of several psychological theories and philosophies is that the way we approach and interpret events in our lives impact how we feel about the events and even define our experience of reality. On the other hand, many people experience a guiding force in their lives, alerting and encouraging them to choose life-affirming options.

From a Christian perspective, God gave us free will *and* has a higher purpose in mind for each of us. As discussed in Rick Warren's book, "A Purpose Driven Life," our job is to understand and get in-line with this purpose and plan. Although I don't think we are ever capable of grasping and holding the entire, complete meaning of our lives, when we more clearly understand our purpose in the world, we can intentionally direct our energies, prayers, and choices in accordance with this deeper understanding. Generally speaking, when our intentions and behaviors are in-line with a spiritually-based sense of purpose, our lives are more joyous, meaningful, and successful.

A Zen Buddhism perspective adds to the discussion of this interplay of free will and determination by espousing concepts such as *flow* and *naturalness*. In "Zen Mind, Beginners Mind," Shunryu Suzuki uses the image of a plant growing naturally out of the ground. "The seed has no idea of being some particular plant, but it has its own form and is in perfect harmony with the ground, with its surroundings. As it grows, in the course of time it expresses its nature...That is what we mean by naturalness." From this perspective, we all have a natural course of development and growth that can flow in our lives. Difficulties occur when our choices are not in accordance with these natural processes and who we really are, when our lives are not being led by the Real Self.

Another way of thinking about free will and determinism is an image of a tunnel. Most people see their lives and options as very narrow, as if contained within a tunnel. They are largely unaware of the many possibilities swirling just outside their tunnel. Fear-based thinking drives this tunnel-vision and defines reality. Conversely, when we embrace love and Spiritual Energy in our lives we become awake to the many possibilities available to us.

Thus, Spiritual Energy seems to offer an *invitation* to live life in accordance with a deeper purpose and meaning; we still have the freedom to choose whether to accept the invitation. Jesus said, "Come to me, all you who are weary and burdened, and I will give you rest."[7] When we accept the invitation and guidance of Spiritual Energy we naturally make life-affirming choices and we experience a flow, congruence, and naturalness in our lives. In short, Spiritual Energy can invite you, but you have to remember to listen and to act courageously on your convictions.

Creativity and Artistic Expression

To what degree do you value the arts and creative expression? What forms of creative arts touch your heart and move you emotionally? Does producing or engaging in artistic creativity lead you to experience a shift in consciousness?

One of the most significant events that impacted my motivation to write this book occurred when I went to a local poetry reading. I have always had an appreciation for the arts and could *see* Spiritual Energy at work in various forms of creative expression, including music and visual arts. However, when I went to this poetry reading I felt as if my heart literally opened up and I experienced clarity about the deep connection between artistic expression and Spiritual Energy. As I was driving home from the reading, I had a very strong sensation of warm light pouring into my chest. I pulled the car over and wept, feeling a profound sense of gratitude for life and the presence of Spiritual Energy in all things. I also experienced a sense of purpose and clarity related to writing this book and to the content of the book. After attending the poetry reading, the outline of the book poured out of me over the next few days. I couldn't quiet the thoughts and ideas unless I wrote them down. I was totally consumed. I went from having a vague interest in writing a book to having the entire book outlined in just five days after the poetry reading.

Creativity and artistic expression are a conduit for Spiritual Energy. The creative process is touched and guided by energy and vision that are transcendent. It is outside normal everyday perception. And, creative arts invite us to experience transcendent glimpses that challenge and expand our ordinary tunnel-vision.

Many of my clients are both deeply spiritual and deeply artistic. They embrace many different faiths. Yet, regardless of their specific spiritual and religious beliefs, the common denominator seems to be a connection between spirituality and the creative process. Many of my clients have read "The Artist's Way," by Julia Cameron. This wonderful and powerful book provides tools and a structure for harnessing our personal, spiritual, and creative potentials. I encourage all of my clients to have some form of regular spiritual and reflective practice in their lives. Many times, creative and artistic expression is an important part of that practice.

Nature and Natural Beauty

Do you see or experience spirituality in nature? Does nature or natural beauty help you reduce your feelings of separation or isolation between you and the world? What do you sense when you look closely at an old tree, light reflecting off water, a snow-covered mountain turning pink during a sunset, or ocean waves breaking against rocks? Do you experience something larger than yourself? Do you have glimpses into spirituality or the nature of reality?

Many people report being deeply affected by nature and indicate that participation in the natural world is the primary way they access and experience spirituality. Connecting with the "Body of the Earth," as Joan Halifax describes in her book, "The Fruitful Darkness," is a sacred and basic aspect of our very existence. Unfortunately, modern life often disconnects us from nature and, therefore, from our core selves. Reconnecting to nature feeds and nourishes our souls and restores perspective in our lives. For some people, intentionally connecting to geography and nature is a form of pilgrimage, whereby, as Joan Halifax says, "the Earth heals us directly."

Recognizing our oneness with nature and the "value of place," as discussed by Rick Bass in his book, "The Book of Yaak," creates a convergence of ecology and spirituality. As Diane Dreher says, "To study nature is to follow the Tao; to follow the Tao is to know ourselves." When we lose touch with nature and natural beauty, we lose touch with ourselves. When intentional engagement with nature is part of our regular spiritual practice, we stay connected to the natural rhythms of life and to Spiritual Energy within and around us.

Open-Heartedness

To what degree are you ruled by your head rather than your heart? How often do you feel an open-hearted connection with others or the world? How often do you allow yourself to be emotionally affected by the magnitude of existence?

Many people describe their experience of spirituality as

deep, very personal, and heart-felt. Some discuss spirituality in intellectual terms. Most, however, describe an experience that transcends words and rational explanations. Spiritual experience tends to be a matter of the heart.

If our hearts are open to the experience, Spiritual Energy changes us. It changes our perceptions of ourselves, others, and reality. How different our reality is when our consciousness is based on a loving heart rather than fear and scarcity. Heart-felt experience leads to a generousness of spirit.

Someone once told me that having children changes you. She said, "Your heart is no longer inside just your body. Part of your heart now resides inside your child." I resonate deeply with this understanding. My heart physically aches when I am not with my children; I long to reconnect our hearts.

Having children certainly provides opportunities to become open-hearted, but it is far from the only way to do so. Heart-felt experience is available to us all the time, in every moment. We often simply forget to notice. We become too busy to awake to the possibilities. We stay task-focused and closed-off from others and our true nature.

When you come home after a long day, does your exhaustion, need to complete tasks, or thoughts about your day interfere with your awareness and ability to be open with your family members or friends in the present moment? If you are closed-off regularly, significant others may have given up on you and stopped hoping you might respond with an open heart. Yet, these moments are some of the most available to assist you in reconnecting with Spiritual Energy and your Real Self. If your relationships are life-affirming, be generous with your spirit. You will be filled in return.

Personal Relationship

Do you have a personal relationship with spirituality? Have you experienced an almost indescribable synergy during certain life-affirming encounters? How often do you open your heart to allow yourself to be touched by as well as to touch others? Have you experienced relationships or encounters that shift your perspective of yourself and the world?

Spirituality is a very personal matter. As I have expressed throughout this chapter, there are many ways to define, know, and experience spirituality. I greatly enjoy talking with my clients about their evolving views of spirituality. Because I am not threatened by different spiritual views and am eager to learn about their insights and experiences, clients generally feel very comfortable expressing themselves and are thankful to have a place to do so. The idea that God meets people where they are, which many Christians believe, describes the personal nature of one's relationship with Spiritual Energy. When we think that we have the only right way to define or know spirituality, we create judgment and divisiveness and inhibit healthy dialogue between faiths. Conversely, an accepting and open approach to the many ways of experiencing spirituality encourages others to discuss their views, which increases our consciousness and awareness of the Spiritual Energy that is available to all of us.

This leads to a related idea: Spiritual Energy occurs most readily within relationships. First, the gifts of spirituality occur when we develop a personal relationship with Spiritual Energy. As a friend and colleague of mine said when I asked her about her definition of spirituality, "It must be personal for it to be transformative." Some form of reflective practice is essential to developing this personal relationship and to keeping the existence of Spiritual Energy in the forefront of our awareness. Regular prayer, for example, fosters this consciousness and provides a format for the development of a personal relationship with Spiritual Energy. A heightened personal awareness of Spiritual Energy then increases the intentionality of our actions; by thinking about it we are more likely to act from a mindset that is informed by Spiritual Energy. Most important, a personal relationship with Spiritual Energy forms the basis of one's own moral barometer and sense of personal integrity. When we lose touch with this personal relationship, the development of our personal integrity is inhibited and we become lost in our lives, an idea that will be expanded upon in the next few chapters.

In addition to developing one's own personal relationship with spirituality, Spiritual Energy occurs within interpersonal relationships. As I have begun to discuss, when we talk about Spiritual Energy we become awake to its existence; it comes alive for those entering into the dialogue. This idea is captured in the words of Jesus, "For where two or three are gathered in my name, there I am in the midst of them."[8]

And, Spiritual Energy seems to operate between people. Many people report strong feelings when they are in the presence of someone who is deeply connected to Spiritual Energy. From a Buddhist perspective, enlightened people, termed Bodhisattvas, are on a personal path of awakening that includes foregoing complete enlightenment in order to help other people on their spiritual journeys. I believe all of us have the ability to be Bodhisattvas, although some are much more connected to Spiritual Energy and a helping role than are others. When we act from a place of connection to Spiritual Energy and in accordance with our personal integrity, we become guides and healers to people around us.

We don't have to be a Bodhisattva to make an impact,

however. When we act in accordance with Spiritual Energy and our personal integrity, we will naturally bring kindness and compassion to those around us. This compassionate energy ripples out and is passed along through relationships. Relationships are also a key to personal healing. Most problems that bring people into counseling or psychotherapy result from disturbances in relationships. Problems oftentimes are rooted in attachment issues with parents and family members and are played out in adult relationships. Along with contributing to problems for many people, relationships are also the primary vehicle for healing. These ideas will be discussed further in later chapters. At this point, suffice it to say that when we are in relationships where the people involved are connected to Spiritual Energy and their personal integrity, great amounts of health and healing are possible. As Charlotte Kasl says in her book, "If the Buddha got Stuck," *Loving relationships heal trauma.*

Thematic Integration

Spirituality is a very personal issue. In this chapter, I outlined some key themes related to understanding, experiencing, and expressing a personally-defined sense of spirituality. Specifically, convergence exists around the importance of *remembering* both inner knowledge and external presence as well as connecting with Spiritual Energy through both transcendent and ordinary experiences. Present moment awareness brings the greatest opportunities for embracing one's Real Self and the accompanying sense of peace and intuitive knowing. Connecting with Spiritual Energy often brings clarity and perspective about the interconnectedness of life, which tends to increase our compassion for others and an awareness of the impact of our thoughts and actions on the world around us.

Spiritual Energy is a loving compassionate force. Embracing love in our lives, rather than fear, brings joy and abundance rather than reactivity and scarcity. Accepting the *invitation* of Spiritual Energy requires active use of our free will and courage to act on our convictions and integrity. Spiritual Energy can be accessed through various forms of reflective practice, including prayer, meditation, creativity and artistic expression, beholding nature and natural beauty, and open-heartedness. Most important, Spiritual Energy is personally-defined and occurs within life-affirming relationships. When we develop a personal relationship with Spiritual Energy we tend to develop a strong sense of personal integrity and to choose interpersonal relationships that are life-affirming.

In the next two chapters I will discuss the various ways that we can become *lost*. Losing touch with Spiritual Energy and our associated personal integrity and wisdom are key aspects related to why we may develop sustained difficulties in our lives.

Chapter 4

Getting Lost: A Psychological Perspective

"I am quite aware that out of defensiveness and inner fear individuals can and do behave in ways which are incredibly cruel, horribly destructive, immature, regressive, anti-social, hurtful. Yet one of the most refreshing and invigorating parts of my experience is to work with such individuals and to discover the strongly positive directional tendencies which exist in them, as in all of us, at the deepest levels."

Carl Rogers, *On Becoming a Person*

Getting lost is about losing touch with who you are at your core, the inner wise person that exists within each of us. The psychological theories discussed in Chapter Two provide insights into why we stop listening to our inner voice of knowledge and clarity, why we stop connecting with and listening to our Real Self.

In accordance with those theories my belief is that the vast majority of psychological problems develop in relational contexts, with families being our first and primary learning environment—our first and primary place of interpersonal learning. As children each of us had nodal and repetitive family experiences that significantly shaped our sense of:

- who we are.

- what we expect from others.
- our role in future relationships.

These family experiences set the stage for the ways we attempt to overcome and master conflicts in our lives as well as the predictable and patterned ways that we get *lost*. The following discussion offers an integrative perspective on some important issues that contribute to our losing touch with our own inner wisdom and associated actualizing potentials.

Role Modeling

Who were your primary role models as a child and adolescent? What types of priorities, values, and behaviors did they emphasize and model? Did anyone teach you to listen to your own inner knowledge?

Many of us were not supported during childhood in developing an inner-directed knowing. We may not have had adult role models who valued intuitive knowledge. Our parents may have been lost themselves and lacked the skills or knowledge related to helping us to develop a stable sense of self. Our parents quite simply may not have known how to be sensitive to the individual needs of their children. In fact, they most likely role modeled many of the behaviors and characteristics discussed in this chapter.

Consequently, as children we didn't learn to turn inward and cultivate and value our own intuitive knowledge and personal power. As adults, we may still lack these skills and have only a faint idea that a Real Self exists within us.

Invalidation

What was the quality of parenting that you received as a child? Were your feelings and experiences acknowledged? Or, were you regularly minimized, disregarded, and told that your feelings and perceptions were wrong?

Sensitive parenting includes validating a child's experiences and unique emotional and cognitive reactions, rather than minimizing or disregarding them. Validation involves recognizing and affirming another person's feelings, thoughts and perceptions, which can be difficult for parents when they don't like their child's reactions. For example, a child may interpret a parent's behavior at any given time as unkind or unfair. Validation would involve acknowledging the child's emotional upset, even if the parent doesn't agree with the interpretation and chooses to redirect the child in some way. Validation provides the important step of recognition and acknowledgment of the child's experience.

Validation helps children develop congruence between their inner and outer worlds. It provides a mirroring process of their experience that assists them with their identity development and self-regulation skills. When children are regularly validated they learn to recognize their feelings, identify who they are, and muster their internal resources. They are able to soothe themselves in the face of adversity and anxiety. Conversely, children who have their realities regularly invalidated tend to have difficulty trusting themselves and lack the ability to self-soothe when they feel anxious.

Marsha Linehan's research documents the effects of an invalidating family environment, especially for a child who is emotionally vulnerable. She found that invalidating environments fail to help children learn to:

- label and modulate emotional arousal. Instead, they have difficulty naming, understanding, or moderating their emotions.
- tolerate distress. Instead, they become overwhelmed

easily and exhibit low levels of frustration tolerance; they struggle with being able to self-soothe in the face of anxiety.

• trust their own emotional responses or perceptions as valid interpretations of events. Instead, they become distrustful of and disconnected from their own emotional reactions; they learn to scan the environment for clues about how to feel and act.

In short, repeated parental invalidation tends to lead to an external versus internal focus, difficulty trusting oneself, and underdeveloped self-soothing skills. Chronic invalidation in childhood is one of the primary reasons that people struggle in their lives and enter psychotherapy as adults.

Consider the following clinical example: Bob came to therapy struggling with depression, failed intimate relationships, and chronic anxiety. Low-level depression and anxiety were with him almost always; periodically these symptoms would increase to the point that he couldn't get out of bed all day. He grew up with a self-centered, alcoholic mother and an inconsistent father; his father was available if Bob succeeded at athletics, but was distant the rest of the time. Bob's feelings and experiences were regularly invalidated; a strong implicit message from both parents was about the importance of maintaining an outer image of being a respectable family while ignoring the obvious problems within the family. Bob tried hard to gain his father's approval and avoid his mother's alcohol-induced anger.

Bob's intimate relationships in adulthood reflected this same pattern: he tended to be in relationships with volatile women and he worked hard to please them and avoid their anger and frustration with him. Yet, these women all complained that he never seemed comfortable with himself; they never felt like the "real Bob" was present. He reported not knowing who he really was. When stressed, which was frequent, Bob would alternate between frantic attempts to please his intimate partner and emotional collapse. He would work overtime to get the approval of others, and then give up with a sense of failure and resignation. Bob had all the tell-tale signs of chronic parental invalidation: a tendency to be a chameleon in his relationships with a tenuous sense of self, constant anxiety and insecurity, and difficulty self-soothing and owning his personal power.

Roles

What was your position or role in your family? Were you the one who was always in trouble? Were you the one who was trying to make other family members laugh? Were you the "good kid?" Were you trying to fix problems or take care of other members? Were you the invisible one, trying to stay out of the way? Do you continue to play the same role(s) in your adult life?

Each of us must find a place in our family. And every family member engages in the interdependent process of being assigned a role or creating a niche in the family system. Right from the birth of their first child, most parents start the process of assigning names and descriptions to their children based on perceived and actual characteristics and behaviors. Johnny is the emotional one. Suzie is the stubborn one. I can always count on Brian to take care of his sister and his mom, etc. Children are labeled and assigned a role in the family largely based on an interaction between actual characteristics that the child possesses and projections from the parents. Projections occur when parents *see* qualities in the child that remind them of someone else (like their own parents) or of parts of themselves. The child may resemble some aspects of the chosen quality, and the parents begin to view the child as if s/he really possesses this quality; the quality becomes equated with the child. Then children start to believe that they are this quality and act accordingly. These projections have the effect of creating a restricted role for children rather than encouraging them to become who they really are. Children adopt the characteristics of the assigned role rather than their Real Self.

Other times, children look out into their families and see a need. They perceive that it's up to them to step into a role, to fill a need. This tends to happen more frequently in families that are not functioning well, where the parents or caregivers are not willing or able to provide effective parenting. Literature and research related to children who grow up in alcoholic and dysfunctional families provide compelling examples of these, at times, overlapping roles:

- The Hero: the child who makes the family look good to outsiders.
- The Caretaker: the child who takes care of others and cleans up their messes.
- The Parent: the child who provides leadership and guidance for the family, even the parents.
- The Scapegoat: the child who diverts attention away from family problems by becoming the focus of negative attention.
- The Sacrificial Lamb: the child who endures abuse so that others will be spared.
- The Lost Child: the child who is invisible and doesn't have needs.
- The Mediator: the child who attempts to achieve peace by negotiating between members.
- The Mascot: the child who distracts members from family problems through humor.

How entrenched these roles become depends on a variety of factors. The most important of which are: (a) the length of time that the child is in the role, (b) the degree of urgency and emotionality that motivates the role, and (c) the degree of pervasiveness of the role. Specifically, when a child is in a role for longer periods of time, with higher levels of emotionality and urgency, and across different contexts, there is a higher likelihood that the child will continue this role into adulthood and that it will be rigid and difficult to change.

When we embrace a rigid role, we move further away from our Real Self. Our sense of self in relationships becomes restricted and limited by the role. Others experience us as a restricted self and treat us accordingly. Thus, we invite others to know and interact with us from this restricted role. Our identity becomes based on the role rather than the natural, life-affirming possibilities of our Real Self.

Structural Family Difficulties

Who had the power in your family when you were a child? Did your parents work together as a team? Did one of your parents have a child as a confidant? Was their a feeling of cohesion and belonging in your family? Did you trust your parents to meet the needs of family members fairly? Did your parents provide a sense of security?

Every family has certain structures that provide the rules of relating among members. Some family structures and associated rules tend to consistently lead to difficulties for children. In particular, the types of boundaries that exist within the family often predict the level of family functioning. Again, boundaries regulate the amount and quality of affiliation and information that flow between family members. Rigid boundaries between members allow for little affiliation and lead to disengaged relationships, which are characterized by emotional distance and lack of intimacy. Diffuse boundaries permit too much affiliation and lead to enmeshed relationships, which are characterized by a lack of separateness and autonomy. Healthy boundaries support affiliation and cohesion as well as independence and autonomy. In other words, healthy boundaries allow children to receive care and support from parents, and also give them a sense of separateness, autonomy, and individuality.

The parental subsystem, also known as the *executive subsystem*, is the foundation of any family with children. The parental subsystem can include biological, adoptive, step, and foster parents as well as others filling parental roles, such as grandparents. Ideally, the parental subsystem provides the leadership and executive decision-making for the family in ways that support healthy functioning of the system and its members. The quality of parenting and type of boundaries around the parental subsystem are the primary predictors of how well a family functions.

In healthy two-parent families, the parental subsystem is a stable alliance. The parents will disagree at times, but they typically provide a unified front and form a collaborative team to support each other with the various tasks of leading a family. The love, limits, and guidance that they provide are fair, reasonable, and age-appropriate. Although this vision for family leadership may sound Pollyannaish or pie-in-the-sky to some people, research has consistently found that a strong parental bond is a fundamental feature of well-functioning families while a poorly functioning parental subsystem is associated with a variety of psychological and behavioral problems in children, teenagers, and adults.

Single-parent families that function well also exhibit a clearly defined executive subsystem that provides leadership for the family. Although it is typical in single-parent families that some executive functions are shared with older children, friends, or extended relatives, an appropriate boundary still exists between children and adults which allows children to feel safe and secure and to know their place in the family. Children need to know that someone is in charge, there are limits to what is permissible, and their needs will be addressed and met.

Boundary problems in families typically result in some form of a *cross-generational coalition.* Cross-generational coalitions occur when the executive subsystem is weak and a parent has a stronger alliance with someone (usually a child) other than the other parent or designated member of the executive subsystem. These coalitions are often seen in families where a parent uses a child as a confidant or refers to the child as "my best friend." This cross-generational alliance, often referred to as *parentification of the child,* gives too much power to the child and typically creates a collusive contract between parent and child: the child will be the parent's confidant and share the parent's emotional burdens; in return, the parent won't play an authoritative role with the child. This dynamic leads to predictable problems for children, such as: struggles with authority and limits in other areas of life, anxiety due to feeling emotionally burdened, and differentiation difficulties due to guilt associated with excessive emotional loyalty to the parent.

Commonly, children who are parentified have an exaggerated sense of self-importance, which covers up underlying feelings of inadequacy. They are often privy to details about the parent's life or relationship(s), including the marriage. Children in these circumstances often feel emotionally responsible for the parent, which leads to feelings of being special or superior. However, because children can't consistently make life (e.g., relationships, finances, and addictions) better for their needy parent, they also feel burdened and inadequate; they simply do not have the experience, knowledge, or abilities to fix their parent's problems. This grandiose sense of responsibility and power as well as underlying fears of inadequacy continue for these children into their adulthood. Alternating between extreme positions of arrogance (i.e., pseudo-confidence) and self-doubt, they are driven to succeed out of a fear of failure or inadequacy. Patterns of enmeshment and externally-focused reactivity in their relationships also persist. They have learned to tune-in and react to another person's pain rather than follow their own inner-voice. The more rigidly they play the role of confidant, savior, or emotional support for another person, the more they can lose touch with who they truly are. The sustainable and unique potential of their Real Self becomes lost in their reactivity and flip-flop between self-doubt and over-confidence.

Differentiation Difficulties

In what ways are you re-living the life of your parents? Do you find yourself replicating interpersonal dynamics or personality characteristics of your parents? To what extent do you aggressively push away aspects of what was role modeled from your parents and family? Does your life feel like your own or an extension of your parents? If you have children, do you see them as reflections of you or your dreams? Can you see your children as separate from you and on their own life journey?

The central developmental task of young adulthood is to embrace a separate sense of self and autonomy while remaining in contact with family members. The differentiation process is a complicated one for parents and children and commonly creates psychological dilemmas for both generations. The key dilemma for children is how to maintain connection with and approval of their parents while being true to themselves. The central issue for parents is how to support their children and allow them to separate and live their own lives. Parents must provide their children with a delicate balance between freedom that encourages their autonomy and guidance that provides support and direction. Young adults must walk the thin line between separating from parents, taking ownership for their own beliefs and choices, and maintaining connection to their families.

Some young adults deal with this balancing act by foregoing their own search process and accepting what parents or caregivers define for them. They remain *fused* with their parents. They do not attain a separate sense of self. They remain in an emotionally reactive and immature position vis-à-vis their parents. In other words, they foreclose on their identity search and blindly accept what has been told to them, without challenging or deciding for themselves. Thus, they become externally-focused and disconnected from their Real Self.

Other young adults deal with the differentiation dilemma by reactively *cutting off* from their families. They resist fusion by pushing against their parents. These individuals are also externally-focused; they are simply reacting against the external demands of their families. They can be just as disconnected from their own sense of self as fused individuals; they cover up their lack of self with reactive identity choices related to relationships or lifestyle while espousing a façade of independence.

The root of fusion and emotional cut off as well as the intensity of their reactions are largely determined by the degree to which children are the recipients of their parents' projected anxiety. The most common form of parental projection occurs when children are triangulated into spousal conflict, which requires the child to choose sides between the parents. Another common process occurs when parents project their own agendas onto the child. Examples include wanting a child to go to a certain school, practice a certain religion, or engage in a certain occupation, based largely on the parent's wishes or experiences rather than on what is truly best for the child. When children experience sustained or high levels of projected anxiety, they have trouble knowing how to regulate their own personal boundaries and tend to be overwhelmed by their own or others' emotions. They have trouble figuring out their own beliefs and lose touch with their core sense of self in the face of others' anxiety, especially that of their parents. To deal with this anxiety, they remain fused with their parents and/or reactively cut off.

Both fusion and cut off result in poorly differentiated young adults without a clear or stable sense of self, who tend to be highly anxious and to internalize the anxiety of others. They have difficulty self-soothing and also tend to alternate between extremes of closeness and distance in relationships. Specifically, they take on others' anxiety as their own or create distance to avoid being overwhelmed by the emotionality of significant others. Stated another way, poorly differentiated adults have trouble embracing the emotional middle ground and the appropriate boundaries needed for healthy relationships. The reactive aspects of differentiation difficulties, therefore, inhibit the development of an inner-directed sense of self, including personal integrity and inner wisdom. Due to the importance that I place on differentiation, a more detailed discussion of the differentiation process and associated characteristics of psychological health will be discussed in Chapter Six.

Guilt

What are the main producers or triggers of guilt in your life? What role does guilt play in your decision-making? To what degree does guilt influence your ability to be true to yourself and take ownership for your life and decisions?

Guilt serves the limited purpose of encouraging people to reflect on their behaviors and the consequences of their words and actions on others. Children are thus socialized to be conscious of the standards set forth by their families and society. At its best, this process helps children internalize these lessons in a balanced way and build their own inner-directed sense of morality and personal integrity.

Unfortunately, guilt has some problems as a socializing agent. The most significant problem with guilt, particularly as a means of control used in parenting, is that it can inhibit the development of an inner-directed sense of integrity and interfere with the identity and differentiation process. Simply said, guilt is most often an externally-imposed energy that keeps us stuck in old, developmentally inappropriate roles, especially when we are trying to assert a separate sense of self.

When exposed to externally-based guilt, children tend to feel disloyal if they express views or engage in behaviors that are deemed unacceptable by their parents and other significant adults. They deal with these feelings of disloyalty by reactively cutting off from parents or by ignoring and minimizing their own thoughts and choices. Either way, the development of their own sense of self and inner knowledge is inhibited and often replaced by ideas that others have for them or with reactivity (i.e., they are reacting against others' ideas rather than truly choosing their own). It is a very difficult choice for some young adults: (a) staying true to their developing sense of self and personal integrity, but giving up the love and approval of parents or significant others and living with feelings of guilt and disloyalty versus (b) gaining the approval of parents or others, but giving up their own core sense of self and living with feelings of inauthenticity and self-alienation.

Trauma

Have you had emotionally, psychologically, or physically painful experiences in your life? What sense have you made of these experiences? Do you blame yourself? Have you experienced symptoms such as anxiety, panic, depression, unwanted disturbing images of the painful events, or hypervigilance? Have you made fear-based attempts to avoid any reoccurrence of these events?

Human beings are meaning makers. We need to make sense of what happens to us so we can predict our world and avoid painful and threatening experiences. According to family systems theory, parents often pass down to their children what was done to them in their own families. Sometimes, what gets passed down is quite traumatic: neglect, emotional and psychological abuse, physical and sexual abuse, and addictions. The consequences of childhood trauma tend to be far-reaching for individuals and their subsequent relationships. Traumatic experiences typically result in low self-esteem, deep-seated fears, and rigid and unhealthy thoughts and behaviors.

When trauma happens to children, they develop beliefs about the trauma based on their level of psychological and cognitive development. Consequently they tend to think they are the cause of their own abuse and that they can control it by changing how they act. So children's beliefs about why traumatic experiences have occurred tend to be self-blaming, leading to rigid rules about how they must act to prevent, avoid, or change the abusive behavior. These rules and associated inflexible behaviors tend to stay with children into adulthood, and oftentimes get reinforced by experiences in adult relationships. When people stay stuck in relational patterns that inhibit them from connecting with their Real Self, their creativity, spontaneity, and joy are greatly diminished.

One fairly consistent effect of trauma is that it teaches children to tune into external cues in their environment rather than into their internal sense of self. They learn to read the environment for signs of danger, staying alert and vigilant to maintain their own or others' safety. Parental or spousal violence is a powerful example of this process. When parents are physically abusive to children or spouses, children learn to read the environment, including their parents, to see if it is safe to engage with the family, especially the abuser. They look externally to determine if they are safe or if they should employ interpersonal strategies to protect themselves or others. Thus they have issues related to safety and control in their subsequent relationships. Like the invalidating environment then, trauma (especially violence and chronic stress) teaches children to scan the environment for clues about how to feel and act. They learn to accept this state of affairs as normal; this is just how life is. Consequently, they lose touch with their own intuitive knowledge and inner-generated personal power and instead, focus almost exclusively on external information and on fear-based attempts to control the environment around them.

Another unfortunate consequence of trauma is that it tends to be replicated throughout a person's life, although the type and intensity of the trauma may change over time. This happens for several reasons. First, the inflexible thoughts and behaviors that

Rick Johnson Ph.D.

are generated as children attempt to understand and cope with the anxiety of traumatic experiences tend to be generalized to all areas of their life and to be self-fulfilling in nature. Specifically, when we approach a new relationship with the same old rigid interpersonal style, others will usually react to our rigidity with a complementary response. For example, controlling interpersonal behaviors tend to attract and elicit obedient and passive responses. Conversely, passive interpersonal behaviors tend to attract and elicit dominating people. Thus, each person's relational expectations are confirmed and reinforced.

People also try to replicate familiar relational styles in an attempt to heal past trauma, disconfirm unhealthy beliefs, and increase behavioral flexibility. By re-enacting past trauma in current relationships we hope better outcomes will occur than what occurred when we were children. This emerges in two ways in adult relationships: (1) we replicate our familiar position in the traumatic experience (e.g., powerless victim), or (2) we re-enact the familiar traumatic dynamic, but take the interpersonal complementary position of the abuser (e.g., angry bully). Either way, we hope the outcome will be different and we will resolve the trauma. Unfortunately, most of the time this repetition compulsion ends up re-traumatizing all involved. And as we stay stuck in our seemingly endless attempts to master the trauma, the balanced and life-affirming energy of our Real Self remains out of our awareness.

De-Selfing

What parts of yourself or your behaviors have you or others deemed unacceptable? What have you done with these unacceptable parts? Do you work hard to gain the approval of others? How successful are you at gaining others' approval, and at what cost to you? Do you rebel against the norms and expectations of others?

Even when there was no obvious trauma in childhood such as physical or sexual abuse, children can learn to *de-self* in their families of origin. Specifically, many children are told and shown they will not be lovable or acceptable unless they act in certain ways. They are not provided the kind of parental guidance that supports the development of their own identity and ownership for their choices. Rather, they are almost exclusively reacting to the demands of the external world by blindly accepting what they are told about themselves and the world or by reactively rebelling against those external demands. Either way, parts of themselves are rejected or split off from their consciousness and not integrated into their core sense of self. As described by Jung, these parts are thus relegated to the *shadow* of their personality.

Most often, children begin this troubling process by minimizing or denying parts of themselves deemed unacceptable by significant adults, such as emotionality, spontaneity, joy, playfulness, and intuitive knowing. Over time, children and adolescents lose touch with these important parts of themselves in an attempt to gain the love and approval of their parents. They trade the intuitive knowing of their inner wisdom for the conditional love of their parents or other adult figures. In other words, they stop listening to their own intuitive knowing and focus on pleasing others and living up to others' definition of values, success, or happiness.

They may believe, for example, that crying is unacceptable or that I'm "ok" only if I have this particular job, house or car, or believe in that particular faith, or marry that particular intimate partner. Losing connection with parts of themselves, especially their intuitive knowing, is especially harmful because it leads to an enduring lack of trust in oneself, the Real Self. This external focus can also lead to excessive perfectionism and associated problems, such as eating disorders, self-criticism, depression, anxiety disorders, and self-injurious behaviors (e.g., cutting or burning oneself).

The flip side of this process occurs when children adopt a rebellious identity or role in their lives. Although a certain amount of testing and challenging the status quo is a natural and healthy part of psychosocial development, it can also become extreme and lead to enduring difficulties. Many times, extreme rebellion is a sign that teenagers and young adults are losing touch with important parts of themselves, namely the parts that are viewed as being aligned with the societal mainstream: productivity, seriousness, honesty, and responsibility. Unfortunately, they also lose touch with their intuitive knowing and sense of what is life-affirming, often engaging in various forms of self-destructive behaviors: underachievement and school failure, substance abuse and addictions, criminal behavior, and self-injurious behaviors. They can become even more alienated from their Real Self than the children who blindly adopt their parents' identities. Either way, children and teens can get psychologically lost, failing to develop a clear inner compass, a sense of their own personal integrity, and knowledge of their Real Self.

Compensatory Strategies

How do you cope with anxiety or situations when you feel threatened? Do you fight or attempt to master the conflict? Do you hide and retreat away from the threat and life? Do you attempt to elicit sympathy or assistance? Are there times when you lose touch with your core sense of self when you adopt interpersonal strategies to protect yourself and meet your needs?

Our Real Self is our natural self; it is who we are supposed to be. When we stop embracing our Real Self, for whatever reason, we replace our natural self-actualizing tendencies with compensatory strategies, usually in an attempt to adapt and accommodate to our environment. We trade our natural self for a compensatory self. Most often, we employ compensatory strategies to specifically deal with trauma and the basic anxiety that is generated when attachment to and approval of parents or significant others is threatened. As I discussed in Chapter Two, the three early compensatory solutions that children utilize to deal with difficult family situations, trauma, and the associated basic anxiety are:

- Moving toward others: reducing anxiety by approaching people and attempting to gain their love and approval.
- Moving away from others: reducing anxiety by avoiding contact with others and their perceived demands.
- Moving against others: reducing anxiety by attempting to control or master others and life's circumstances.

These strategies are truly compromise solutions. They are not as healthy and life-affirming as behaviors that are led by the Real Self. They are compromises to accommodate and adapt to unfavorable life circumstances and to make the best of the situation. Unfortunately, they tend to become patterned and employed far longer than the original threats or blocks required. These childhood strategies become our automatic ways of relating and attempting to meet our needs as adults. They help us alleviate anxiety and meet our needs to some degree, but are not sustainable. So, we trade the natural, life-affirming wisdom of the Real Self for the fear-based, automatic reactions of compensatory strategies.

Returning to the example of Bob will help illustrate this process. Bob's primary compensatory solution was to move toward others. He worked hard to read other people, especially his intimate partner, so he could meet her needs, gain her approval, and avoid her anger. Used to excess, which Bob did, this strategy is doomed to failure. As often happens to those who persistently use this strategy, his partner took Bob for granted, expected more and more, and was rarely completely satisfied with his efforts.

Eventually, Bob would employ his next most used strategy: moving away from others. The realization that he had been negating and disallowing his own needs in an unsuccessful attempt to please his partner would land on him like a sledgehammer. He would become emotionally exhausted, depressed, and filled with self-deprecating thoughts. He would withdraw into himself and shut down his contact with others. His withdrawal was met with confusion and anger by significant others, especially his intimate partner. The angrier she became, the more he withdrew.

The complement to Bob was his partner, Julie. Julie also grew up in an alcoholic family. She was the "black sheep" of the family, the one who refused to play by the rules. She was the "truth-keeper" of her family, often commenting on the other members' denial and avoidance of the family dysfunction. Her primary compensatory strategy was moving against others. She was angry much of the time. She experienced Bob's moving toward relational style as disingenuous and superficial. He never seemed to be truly present with her. When he would withdraw, she experienced abandonment and rejection. Like Bob did, she would periodically collapse in depression, shame, and resignation. Eventually, she would return to a place of blaming Bob for her suffering and loneliness.

Bob's compensatory strategies triggered Julie's and vice-versa. His attempts to please her were seen as disingenuous and his withdrawal was experienced as abandonment; both triggered her anger. Her anger triggered his reactive attempts to please her and his withdrawal; and around and around they went. Both felt somewhat more balanced outside of the relationship. Within it, they were locked in a repetitive, complementary cycle which left each of them frustrated and disempowered. They were drowning in their compensatory strategies and restricted roles vis-à-vis each other. Their connection to their Real Self, which was already distant due to childhood experiences, faded even more within their relationship.

Thematic Integration

From a psychological perspective, getting lost occurs when the development of an inner-directed sense of self is compromised or inhibited. The most common ways people get lost psychologically are:

- not being supported or guided in developing a strong, inner-directed moral compass.
- learning to look externally rather than trusting one's intuitive knowing.
- having one's emotions and experiences regularly invalidated.
- playing roles rather than being led by the Real Self.
- growing up in families with poor boundaries, including cross generational coalitions and parentification of children.
- experiencing difficulties with the differentiation process: remaining fused or reactively cutting off.
- experiencing excessive guilt or family loyalty that inhibits the identity and differentiation process.

- experiencing traumatic events.
- learning to minimize or deny parts of oneself.
- developing rigid and unhealthy beliefs about oneself or the world.
- developing rigid and unhealthy behavior patterns or strategies, especially relationship patterns.

Families are the primary place where we learn about ourselves and map out the blueprint of our roles and expectations in relationships. Families are the primary place where we learn life lessons, struggled to attain the balance of separation and togetherness in relationships, and learn interpersonal strategies for managing anxiety. Families are the primary place where our Real Self can flourish or is inhibited in its development. When our development becomes based predominately on factors other than our Real Self, a compromise is initiated whereby the voice of our Real Self becomes more and more faint. Whatever the reason, when we move away from our Real Self, we lose touch with our inner guide. We suffer when our lives are not in-line with and led by our Real Self. Eventually, we will feel depressed, anxious, powerless, unsatisfied, and generally as though we are spinning our wheels, especially in relationships. Over time we will lose touch with our personal integrity and personal barometer of health, and even who we really are.

Chapter 5

Getting Lost: A Spiritual Perspective

"In your longing for your giant self lies your goodness: and that
longing is in all of you. But in some of you that longing is a
torrent rushing with might to the sea, carrying the secrets of
the hillsides and the songs of the forest. And in others it is a flat
stream that loses itself in angles and bends and lingers before it
reaches the shore."
Kahlil Gibran, *The Prophet*

If you believe, as I do, that Spiritual Energy is available to
all of us all of the time, then getting lost spiritually is really like
forgetting. When we are lost, we forget that guidance and support
are available. We forget to trust our inner wisdom or to connect
with and be nourished by life-affirming relationships and activities. When we lose touch with a centered sense of ourselves, we
become disconnected from a spiritual sense of the world. When
we forget to touch Spiritual Energy in our lives, we often forget:

- who we truly are.
- our personal definition of health.
- our essential values.
- our priorities.
- our personal integrity.
- our sense of interconnection and place in the world.
- our connection with our Real Self.

Rick Johnson Ph.D.

When we are lost spiritually, we lose perspective, focus, and most importantly our essential connection to our core self. We forget to open our hearts to the life-affirming energy and knowledge that exists within and around us. Much of the pain that lands people in a psychotherapist's office is associated with people feeling lost and disconnected in their lives and forgetting to touch their inner wisdom and their own spirituality. Consequently, much of what I do in psychotherapy involves helping people to remember who they are and to create structures in their lives that support them so their *hearts and souls can sing.*

I think of the Real Self as our guide and our conduit to Spiritual Energy. Thus, the psychological necessity of connecting to the Real Self is also a spiritual necessity. The Real Self is the Holy Spirit that resides within us. It is God's life breath. It is our Buddha nature, our inner essence and true nature. When we lose touch with the Real Self, we lose touch with the single most important guiding force in our lives, and as a result, we struggle.

Why We Get Lost

Do you live your life based on your core values? Have you developed a sense of ownership and balance of priorities in your life? Or, do you become so busy with life that you forget to be kind and compassionate with others? Does your life lack a sense of meaning and purpose? Are you so busy thinking about what you are going to do next that you are not of aware of what you are doing in the present moment?

It is so easy to get lost. It is so easy to lose touch with Spiritual Energy and a centered sense of self. There are many reasons why this is so. Although not an exhaustive list, the following are a few common reasons and experiences.

First, many people have had negative and reactive experiences with organized religion and with organizations that are proponents of various forms of spirituality. Negative experiences may include abuse, condemnation, and the propagation of fear, guilt, or any ideology that attempts to restrict human potentials and growth, what could be termed, *spiritual violence.* After having an aversive experience, people are wise to withdraw from that particular organization. Unfortunately, they also tend to withdraw from the idea of spirituality in general and, more specifically, the existence of loving, guiding Spiritual Energy.

A second common reason for becoming lost spiritually is fear. This includes not only fear of being hurt or violated spiritually by an organization, but also fear of change. Many clients talk about the fear that if they embrace their emerging awareness of Spiritual Energy in their life, it will require them to live their lives differently. Often, they are not sure what the changes will be. For many people, it feels like a *pull* that is interpreted with moral imperatives: to pray, to go to church, to stop drinking, to be a better person, etc. The moralistic interpretation embedded in this feeling can be quite overwhelming and often triggers past negative feelings associated with organized religion. Consequently, they avoid the awareness that there may be something more to life, something spiritual.

The third typical reason that we become spiritually lost is excessive rationalism. In my view, excessive rationalism occurs when empirical knowing and intellectual thought are held up as the only valid ways of attaining knowledge. Faith-based, experiential, and intuitive forms of knowing are seen as inadequate and unacceptable. This view is often accompanied by condescending views of faith and of any belief systems that can't be proven through the scientific method. The core of this belief is that science will eventually find the answers to all of life's mys-

teries, thereby rendering spiritual views as archaic and unnecessary. Excessive rationalism, then, leads to the acceptance of and
absolute faith in science, and the dismissive view of spiritual faith
and other forms of knowing.

Lastly, people often become lost spiritually because of the
disorienting nature of living in our modern world. Life is assaultive. We are assaulted by noise, environmental pollution, com-
mutes, news of violence and fear, demands of jobs, pressures from
others' needs, etc. We are even assaulted by the pressures of our
own needs. Many of us also feel assaulted by the nagging awareness that there has to be something more meaningful than our
current state of life. "There must be something better. If only I
had the time to figure out what I really want to do or how I really
want to live my life."

Most people wake up every morning and go about their
day in a reactive frame of mind. They react to the dog needing
to be walked, to the kids needing to be dressed and fed, to the
clock telling them that they will be late for work again, to their
partner's desire to have a serious conversation, to the sticker on
their windshield telling them that they are overdue for an oil
change, to the plethora of emails in their inbox, to the blinking
light or beeping on their cell phone indicating unanswered voice-
mails, to the lists of work projects, to the lists of home projects,
to their realization that they haven't exercised in 5 days, to the
latest sensationalized national news story, to the reality of the
brutality of war and terrorism and the associated fear that it generates, and to the up-coming dentist appointment that they have
accidentally double-booked with a business meeting, to name just
a small few.

When we become reactive to the world, it is easy to lose

touch with our priorities, to feel confused, and to lose a sense of clarity about what is important. We feel anxious and disorganized, as though we will never get a handle on our lives. In the face of all this, it is so easy to lose our core sense of self, our Real Self.

Being Spiritually Lost

The following are several predictable consequences that I see again and again in people who have lost touch with their Real Self and associated Spiritual Energy in their lives. I don't mean to imply that once you become awake to Spiritual Energy, you automatically achieve a state of blissful calm. The assaultive nature of life makes it very difficult to maintain a sustainable connection to one's core self and to Spiritual Energy. That is why it is essential to have some form of spiritual practice, which helps us to regularly remember who we are and that Spiritual Energy is available to us. When we forget to connect with our Real Self and Spiritual Energy, even temporarily, the following are very likely consequences; they are predictable markers of when we get spiritually lost.

Reactive Movement

How often are you more focused on the completion of a task than on the enjoyment of the process? Do you work very hard then periodically collapse in exhaustion? How does being task-focused help and hinder your life?

Besides being a reason for getting lost, reactivity is a marker that indicates we have become spiritually lost. Life is chaotic and ripe for reactivity. Many people simply react and react and react, all day every day. They don't slow down and recharge and reflect—there's no time to do so. They never get to a place of being proactive, only reactive. They go from one task to the next to the next. They have stopped listening to their intuitive voice telling them about balance and moderation. They don't read the signs of stress and burn-out until their bodies start breaking down: back aches, extreme tension head aches (minor ones can be ignored or medicated), stress-related illness, etc. They can literally work themselves to death.

The old adage of slowing down and smelling the roses is simplistic, yet so important and so often ignored. There is a time for activity and a time for quiet stillness, "spiritual stillness," as Mary Ann Williamson[1] calls it. When acting from a reactive place we move away from our inner knowledge. Spiritual stillness is a time when we see the beauty in nature, reflect on what is meaningful in our lives, and connect with our intuitive knowledge.

While some people very rarely slow down, others try to recharge during vacations one or two times a year. They relax and unwind in discreet time frames; they compartmentalize stressful situations and relaxing ones. Sometimes, they even fill these vacation times with more reactive movement, albeit not work-related activities. Although some vacation time is better than none, I think it is vital to make spiritual stillness a part of everyday life. Spirituality is not something that just happens in a house of prayer or during worship. Opportunities to be awake to and embrace Spiritual Energy are available every moment, every day. Embracing Spiritual Energy requires slowing down and remembering to be aware of its existence and to accept the invitation to have it touch your heart.

Thinking, Thinking, Thinking
How often are you lost in your thoughts? Is the content

of your thoughts mainly about the past? Or, are you focused on what you need to do in the future? How often do you have the experience of *just being?*

A big part of losing touch with our Real Self and associated Spiritual Energy occurs when we are thinking, thinking, thinking. Most of our thinking-time is spent on what has happened and what will or should happen. As Eckart Tolle points out in his book, "The Power of Now," reality is always in the present. When we spend the majority of our mental time in the past or future, we are living a life that is out-of-touch with reality—reality only exists *in the now.*

Thus, the fastest way to lose touch with your Real Self is to be excessively thinking about the past or the future. This type of thinking brings almost constant suffering. For most of us, our brains can trick us into thinking that we are OK if only we could change the past or if we could get or become something new or different. We simply can't change the past, no matter how much we focus our thoughts on it; we suffer with our inability to change what has happened. In terms of future-oriented thoughts and behaviors, if we succeed at capturing a prized new condition, we soon discover that the satisfaction is short-lived. We quickly experience the void that is created in the wake of attainment, and we begin the search again. Our needs and the context of our life change. Our thoughts move to new conditions that we believe will make us happy or satisfied. We continue to feel a sense of lack, of something missing that is not here right now.

The good news is that the fastest way to reconnect with the Real Self and associated Spiritual Energy is to have present moment awareness. Turning off our brains and being present with our experience in the here and now creates a shift in consciousness. Instead of our consciousness being filled with what should have happened or what needs to happen, we are awake to what is happening. We shift from absence to abundance. The present moment is full of abundance whereas the past and future tend to be about wishing for what is not really here now. When we have mindful awareness in the present moment we remember and reclaim the wisdom and peace of Spiritual Energy, which is available to us every moment.

Tyranny of the List

Do you make lists of things you want to do or accomplish? If yes, what is the impact of your lists on your state of being? Do your lists help or detract from your ability to be connected with a sense of adequacy and peace?

Many of us make lists of things we would like to accomplish or don't want to forget. At its best, list-making is a cognitive support. It helps us remember important activities or tasks we can't do at the moment. We can let go of the need to hold those thoughts in our minds; we can put them on paper and free up brain space for present activities. Unfortunately, instead of being supportive, lists can take on a life of their own and become life-detracting. For many of us, the list becomes a producer of anxiety and a reminder of personal inadequacy. This is what I call, the *tyranny of the list.*

The list becomes a tyrant, an oppressive agent in your life. It symbolizes a sense of lack, that you and your life are inadequate in their current state. The list becomes a reminder of what needs to be done, changed, or fixed. Similar to excessive thinking about the past or future, we often can't be OK until the items on the list are completed. Yet, lists tend to rarely be completed, and many times they grow. Or if they are completed, a new list is soon created. The tyranny of the list never ceases, robbing us of spontaneity and present moment awareness. Lists can rob us of feeling that we and our life are fine, just as they are. We feel anxious and incomplete instead of full and whole. So, what could be a life-supporting tool becomes a detractor of our connection with Spiritual Energy and our sense of fullness and adequacy.

Losing Balance

How do you manage anxiety? Do you engage in addictive or excessive behaviors? To what degree do you become disconnected from your body and present moment experience under stress?

Balance is one of the most important aspects of successful living. The assaultive nature of life, which sends many people into a reactive mode of operating in the world, also triggers feelings of discontent and unease. These feelings of unease themselves lead to a feeling of being out-of-balance with one's natural state of being. We lose touch with our Real Self and feel outside of ourselves. To deal with this, many people resort to extremes. They work, exercise, eat, drink alcohol, engage in sex, and do just about anything to excess in order to feel better. Unfortunately, this only leads to greater feelings of being unbalanced.

Spiritual Energy, in contrast, invites and encourages us to return to our bodies and to a sense of balance in our lives. Moderation truly is the spice of life. The Buddha espoused *the middle path*, which focuses on moderation and balance. When we remember to be awake to Spiritual Energy, we remember to breathe and return to our bodies. Our personal power is cultivated when we stay within ourselves rather than being externally reactive. As I have said, it is essential to have some form of spiritual practice to help us regularly remember who we are, so we can stay connected to a balanced sense of self, our Real Self.

Rick Johnson Ph.D.

Incongruence

How much of your time is spent on activities that are congruent with your core values versus being robotic and mindless? How do you treat others when you encounter obstacles and struggles in your life? Is there a discrepancy between what you do and what you espouse as your core values?

When we lose touch with our Real Self, we lose touch with our inner guide. Consequently, we can lose touch with a core sense of our own morality and personal integrity. There is, at least periodically, incongruity between what we say and what we do, which leads to others having difficulty fully trusting us and our motives. Especially when life doesn't go our way, we can become self-centered; we can forget that how we act really matters and that our actions affect others.

Spiritual Energy helps us remember to live in accordance with our higher self. Regular spiritual practice reminds us of what is important: relationships, family, and values such as honesty and compassion for others. Spiritual Energy helps us to foster these inner-directed values and convictions. When we are clear about who we are and what is important, success is not based on what happens to us, but on how we conduct ourselves. We realize that our actions impact others and can have a ripple effect in our life and the world.

Fighting Against

Are you regularly frustrated and disappointed with your life? Do you feel as if you're swimming upstream? Or, do you experience a sense of flow, meaning, and congruency in your life?

When we lose touch with our Real Self, we lose contact with the meaning and flow of life. Instead of embracing the natural flow of our life, we fight against ourselves and others. Life

94

feels very hard, like banging your head against a wall. Unfortunately, rather than stepping back and returning to a centered sense of self, many people continue to bang away using the same old strategies that are working only moderately well, if at all.

As Joan Halifax points out, some Native Americans refer to God as the *energy-between-things*. This view of spirituality is supported by advances in quantum physics, which describes life as containing a complex web of energy that flows within and between all things and defines our experience of reality. There is a natural flow to life. When we are centered and in touch with Spiritual Energy, our lives feel in-flow. When we act in accordance with the inner wisdom of our Real Self, we are happier, less anxious, and attain a rhythm to our lives that feels right. We are awake and open to giving and receiving messages and experiences from others, often spontaneously.

Fear

Do you worry excessively about your or others' safety? Do you regularly experience a sense of dread? To what degree do you allow your fears to limit your activities?

Fear is a major cause of becoming spiritually lost as well as a marker. People who have lost touch with Spiritual Energy worry a lot. They tend to think that life is more dangerous and more unmanageable than it truly is. They seem to stay in a constant state of fight or flight. Most of the time, they are fleeing. They are fleeing from relationships, challenges, new experiences, and the perceived threats that can be anywhere. Their fear not only restricts their actions and options, but robs them of joy, compassion, and love. They are so busy protecting themselves that they are not open to life-affirming relationships and experiences. Sometimes couched in intellectual thought, their decisions tend to be made based on avoidance of threats rather than what might be actualizing for them and make their hearts sing. As Maryann Williamson points out, fear truly is the opposite of love. Love is the guiding emotion of Spiritual Energy. Fear, on the other hand, is a thief that robs people of spontaneity, freedom, and joy.

Scarcity

In your family growing up, was there a feeling of security that, although not perfect, needs of the members would be met? Or, did you experience scarcity and competition to meet needs? In your current life, do you regularly worry about not having enough (money, love, material things, etc.)?

Spiritual Energy brings *abundance thinking*. People who embrace Spiritual Energy tend to feel like they are living a rich existence: relationships, activities, work, and meaning. They feel a deep sense of gratitude for the blessings in their lives, which tends to bring more gifts and blessings. Catherine Ingram writes, "Gratitude is a precursor to delight. To be truly happy is to live in gratitude."

People who have lost touch with Spiritual Energy tend to see themselves as never having enough. They are fearful that they are not good enough. They operate from the belief that when other people receive, it must be at their expense. Life becomes a competition to get whatever crumbs they can.

This thinking, which I term the *scarcity model*, runs the show in families who have lost their way. In families where abuse and neglect are occurring, the children usually compete with each other for the limited resources and love that are available. Rather than support each other, family members demean or overpower each other in an attempt to meet their own needs. Children who grow up in families in which the scarcity model operates tend to have difficulty visualizing their potentials or believing that they can make changes in their lives. Sadly, when the scarcity model operates, people act in ways that actually move them farther away from abundance and gratitude. Their existence is defined by not having "enough," and acting from this position brings more scarcity rather than less.

Losing Perspective on Suffering

What is your perspective on suffering? Do you see it as an inevitable part of living life? Do you believe that suffering provides opportunities to learn and grow? To what degree do you believe you have control over your own and others' suffering?

Suffering is part of life. It is the first of the Buddha's Four Noble Truths. People who have embraced Spiritual Energy in their lives through some form of regular practice tend to have a much healthier perspective on suffering than those who do not. A regular spiritual practice encourages people to realize that suffering is not only unavoidable, but can bring great insights and life learning. Every struggle and hardship can teach us something about compassion. Hardships provide us with opportunities to experience parts of ourselves and have a deeper understanding of the human condition. I can honestly say that each of the difficult experiences that I have had in my life have contributed to me being a more compassionate and effective psychotherapist. It's not that I search out pain and suffering per se, it's just part of life.

People who are removed from Spiritual Energy in their lives tend to see suffering as a terrible burden that has no purpose. They either try to excessively control their lives in a futile attempt to avoid suffering or they feel powerless in the face of suffering. Either way, they are in pain and have few effective tools to deal with the pain.

Rick Johnson Ph.D.

Sleepwalking

Are you awake in your life? Do you feel a sense of vitality and passion? Or, does your life feel robotic and boring? Do you feel as if your life is your own?

Connection to Spiritual Energy brings passion and excitement for being alive. When we embrace Spiritual Energy the world shifts: similar to shifting from experiencing the world in black-and-white to full color, literally shifting from sleepwalking to living life fully. We come alive. Our hearts open to experiences, relationships, risks, spontaneity, fun and a variety of feelings, especially love. We become open to creative expression and natural beauty. We start to see Spiritual Energy everywhere: artistic creations, nature, forms, light, faces, suffering, grace, kindness, compassion, etc. When we are awake to the present moment, we can embrace the Spiritual Energy that exists within and around us, and we come alive.

Existential Vacuum

Do you know why you are alive? Does your life have purpose? What are your core values? What do you do with your freedom? Does the awareness of being free create anxiety for you? Do you feel like you live a real, authentic life? Do you live your life based on your own or others' values and demands?

Many people feel overwhelmed by these kinds of questions, especially those who are not grounded spiritually. An existential vacuum occurs when someone is lacking a core sense of meaning, a sustainable sense of meaning. People attempt to fill this void of meaning in many different ways, some ways being much more life detracting than others: drugs, alcohol, sexual or relationship addictions, overworking, sport or activity addictions, etc. They compulsively race to fill the void of meaning and try to cover up the anxiety and discontent that it engenders. They define their lives and themselves through activities and avoid listening to and learning from the anxiety which is generated by the faint voice that reminds them there is more to life than they are realizing and they are not living a fully alive and authentic existence.

In contrast, Spiritual Energy exudes meaning. When we embrace Spiritual Energy we become much clearer about why we are alive and how we impact the lives of those around us and the world, and the many ways that we could be more impactful. Spiritual Energy brings a sense of purpose and importance to our life. And meaning is available on a moment-to-moment basis. Each moment offers an opportunity to live life in accordance with a higher self, our Real Self. Each moment offers an opportunity to feel a sense of personal integrity and to live a life of joy and pride. Each moment offers the opportunity to embrace an authentic, balanced sense of self that is full of possibilities and open to the experience of living. Spiritual Energy invites us to become awake and live our lives fully.

Unbalanced Responsibility

What are you responsible for in your life? What can you control? Do you believe that you are powerless to affect change in your life? Or, do you believe that you can influence all aspects of your life through your thoughts, intentions, and actions? Have you found a balance between these extremes?

A long time ago I heard a popular story about a man trapped on top of his house by flood water. He prayed for God to save him. When people in a boat came by to save him, he told them that he is waiting for God, although the water continued to rise. When people in a helicopter flew over to save him, he again told them that he is waiting for God. After he drowned, he asked

God why He didn't come to save him. God said, "Who do you think sent the people in the boat and the helicopter?"

Finding a balance between letting go and taking charge is enormously important to healthy and successful living. Connection to Spiritual Energy seems to give people insights into this balance, enabling them to neither under- or over-estimate the control that they have in their lives. Our Real Self provides guidance about the limits of our responsibility and our personal boundaries.

Recently, a client told me about several dreams that she had in which she was under a great deal of stress and dealing with dangerous circumstances. In one dream, she curled up in a ball in her closet, feeling powerless to influence the circumstances causing her fear. In another dream, she had super-human powers; she was flying above the circumstances, warning others of the impending danger. These dreams depict the two extremes of perception that we tend to use: too little or too much control. Both positions misjudge the degree of control and power that we have to influence the circumstances of our lives. Again, the ability to navigate in-between these two extremes and achieve a balanced view of our personal power is a key aspect to healthy living.

I often use the image of a small boat on a rough, wide-open sea to represent the struggle to find balanced responsibility and control in our lives. Life and all its conditions are the ocean currents, waves, and winds, which have the power to push us around and knock us about. We are the small boat, with a sail and a rudder. We are no match for the waves during a storm. Yet, we have some ability to steer and to stay afloat. In calm seas, we can sail with intentionality and purpose, especially when we utilize the natural flow of the currents and winds. The often used Serenity

Prayer captures this balance that is so difficult to achieve.

God, grant me
the serenity to accept the things I cannot change,
the courage to change the things I can, and
the wisdom to know the difference

Alienation

Do you feel as if you have a purposeful and meaningful place in your world, with family, friends, and community? Do you have a compassionate and empathic connection with others? Or, do you feel disconnected from those around you? If yes, does this lack of meaningful connection lead to feelings of discouragement and emotional fatigue?

People who are disconnected from Spiritual Energy in their lives typically see themselves as separate from other people and their world whereas spiritually-grounded people tend to see themselves as interconnected with all of life. Understanding that we are connected with all people and things engenders compassion and ownership for our world and leads to a sense of being a steward, a Shepard of all that is around us. It leads to the understanding that our behaviors and thoughts truly matter.

Not being in touch with Spiritual Energy, conversely, leads to a disconnection from others and to feelings of alienation and discouragement. When we are spiritually disconnected from all that is around us we feel alone, even when surrounded by others. As I previously stated, Spiritual Energy occurs most readily within relationships. First and foremost, it is foundational to develop a personal relationship with Spiritual Energy. This personal relationship forms the basis of one's own moral barometer and sense of personal integrity and wholeness. When we lose touch with this personal relationship, the development of our personal integrity is inhibited and we become lost in our lives.

Spiritual Energy operates between people. When we act from a place of spiritual connection in accordance with our personal integrity, we open our hearts to how Spiritual Energy can come alive in our relationships. Relationships are the key to healing trauma, to supporting health in our lives, and to building structures that will support sustainable happiness. When we get in-line with Spiritual Energy in our lives, we know which relationships are life-affirming. We gravitate toward others that will support our health. And, others will be drawn to our health and centered energy.

Thematic Integration

Getting lost occurs when we forget to embrace the wisdom, guidance, and life-affirming energy of the Real Self. When this happens we don't embrace the Spiritual Energy that is available to us. When we forget to embrace this presence, we get caught up in minutia in our lives and lose perspective on our values and priorities. We end up losing touch with our personal integrity and personal barometer of health. The consequences of getting lost spiritually are many, including:

- engaging in reactive movement without spiritual stillness.
- losing touch with present moment awareness.
- losing touch with a balanced and centered sense of self.
- feelings of incongruity and a lack of personal integrity.
- fighting against the natural rhythm and flow of life.
- engaging in fear-based living.
- being led by the scarcity model instead of abundance

and gratitude.

- losing perspective on the nature of suffering.
- sleepwalking rather than embracing a zest for life.
- experiencing a lack of meaning and purpose.
- under- or over-estimating the ability to control or influence others or life circumstances.
- experiencing separateness and disconnection from relationships, including from Spiritual Energy itself.

Thankfully, Spiritual Energy is available every moment, and our Real Self provides the avenue for experiencing it. When we embrace our Real Self, we attain clarity on not only our lives, but on larger spiritual perspectives. We remember and connect with deep pools of understanding, which lead to sustainable spiritual and psychological health.

Chapter 6
Psychological Health: Differentiation of Self

"Many supposed attempts at self-definition are really attempts to get others to change or to pry oneself loose from emotionally intense situations."

Michael Kerr, *Chronic Anxiety and Defining a Self*

If psychological and spiritual problems are like getting lost, maybe health is like being found, or finding something, maybe something that has been there all the time. In fact, it is. Psychological health is about finding your Real Self, and embracing it. Psychological health is about allowing your Real Self to guide and lead your life based on a sense of personal integrity, confidence, and "thoughtfully determined direction."[1]

Throughout this book I discuss various theories that point to the psychological necessity of connecting to our Real Self as well as various reasons why we lose touch with its guidance. I have yet to fully describe what happens when we embrace our Real Self. In this chapter, I will talk about the characteristics of psychologically healthy individuals. The discussion will be organized around the concept of *differentiation of self*. It is my belief that differentiation of self, more than any other psychological concept, captures the elements and characteristics associated

Rick Johnson Ph.D.

with the healthy psychological functioning that occurs when we embrace our Real Self. Along with a clinical practice focused on assisting clients in their attempts to become healthier and to increase their differentiation levels, for years I have been conducting research on differentiation of self, including characteristics of high and low levels of differentiation, what leads to higher or lower levels of differentiation, and how differentiation is related to various aspects of psychological health. Let's begin with a discussion of the differentiation process.

The Differentiation Process

We all grow up in a family system, be it biological, nuclear, extended, blended, adopted, foster, or some other kind of residential group. Within the family, each young child begins a process of attaching to and separating from caregivers (usually parents), which is the central dynamic of the differentiation process. Parents experience a mirror process of attachment to and separation from children, largely based on the developmental needs of their children. In other words, healthy development occurs when parents and children form a solid attachment bond and also maintain enough psychological space between them to allow children to develop independence and autonomy, both psychologically and physically.

The differentiation process is a life-long journey for children and parents, with recent research indicating that high levels of differentiation aren't typically achieved until adult children are 30-40 years of age! The emphasis during infancy is on forming a strong attachment; infants are completely dependent upon their parents to care for all their basic needs. As children grow, they quickly begin to express their needs for self-reliance and autonomy, in addition to attachment with parents. Managing this delicate balance effectively requires sensitive parenting. Parents must read their children and respond with parenting that alternately, and sometimes simultaneously, provides love and support as well as opportunities for the child to develop autonomy and mastery. In order to develop a healthy sense of self and their abilities, children need many opportunities to wrestle with tasks that are frustrating while feeling support, rather than over-involvement, from their parents. This dialectical balance of connection with and separation from parents continues unabated throughout childhood, with children typically requiring more independence as they age.

The push-pull of this experience comes to a head during a variety of developmental stages, with adolescence and young adulthood having the potential to become a family battleground. Young adults typically press for high levels of independence and autonomy from parents, propelled by their need to form a separate sense of self and identity, intimate peer relationships, and independence related to work and finances. They are forming opinions and acting upon choices related to values, ideologies, lifestyles, relationships, and careers with varying levels of parental involvement. Some young adult children want more parental involvement in this process while others want less. At this stage, parents are engaged in a balancing act that requires them to encourage autonomy in their young adult children while also being available for mentoring.

Many parents find it excruciatingly difficult to support their children if they perceive that they are making poor choices. This is one place where projection rears its dysfunctional head. In fact, projection is the main culprit when the differentiation process goes poorly. Projection typically occurs when parents act as if their children are extensions of themselves; either consciously or unconsciously, the parents live through their children. In other words, whatever is unresolved for parents is projected onto the children. For example, if a parent was unable to attain a certain life-goal or occupation because of pressure from his/her own parents or due to life circumstances, that parent may demand that his/her children attain that specific goal or occupation. Similarly, if a parent was forced into a certain occupation (e.g., a woman forced to be a nurse when she wanted to be a medical doctor), the parent may demand that her children avoid that specific occupation (i.e., a nurse).

In addition to career choices, this kind of process can occur related to all aspects of identity development and lifestyle, such as religious or spiritual practices, choice of intimate partners, thoughts about having children, and decisions about where to live. All parents have hopes and wishes for their children. The more those hopes and dreams are based upon the parents' own unresolved issues, the more problems are likely to develop. In situations with high levels of projection, children need to react to not only their own struggles and competing agendas, they must also contend with the psychically intrusive quality of their parents' unresolved desires and agendas. Consequently, children often become flooded with indecision and identity-based questions: "Do my parents approve of my choices related to marriage, children, religious faith, education, occupation...?" Parents can also be consumed by complementary questions and thoughts: "I love my children, but their choices make me angry and worried. I know its their life, but how can I support them when they are making the wrong choices?" Children often must choose between doing what they think their parents will approve of versus doing what they think will make themselves happy; either way they are reacting to the psychically intrusive forces of their parents' agendas.

I once worked with a family in which the mother had been forced by her mother to attend a certain university. When she had children, she all but refused to allow her own daughter to attend that same university ("You can go anywhere except to *that* school"). Of course, her daughter made the emotionally-charged choice and went to the forbidden university! Then, the mother had to decide if she was going to reactively withdraw her emotional and financial support of her daughter. Or, the mother could let her daughter make her own choices, which would require that the mother work through her unresolved issues with her own mother.

The consequences of difficulties with the differentiation process were discussed in Chapter Four and are fairly predictable. To summarize, one consequence is that young adult children remain *fused* with their parents. In this case, young adults do not engage in their own identity process; rather, they adopt the identity markers (e.g., education, career, relationships, religious faith, etc.) that their parents define for them. They tend to become externally-focused and disconnected from their own inner wisdom; they don't want to risk parental disapproval by asserting their own ideas and needs. Another typical consequence is *emotional cut off*. In this case, young adults reactively remove themselves from their parents' influence, which is seen as too toxic or threatening to their emerging identity. Lack of parental mentoring and support as well as high levels of reactivity are aspects of cut offs, which tend to make thoughtful decision-making and the attainment of life-goals less likely.

The most unsettling aspect of differentiation difficulties is it tends to be passed down through the generations, what is called the *multigenerational transmission process*. Specifically, the differentiation level of parents is passed down to their children through projection and role modeling. Then, poorly differentiated young adults choose intimate partners with similar levels of differentiation, and then pass down their differentiation levels and processes to their own children.

Thankfully, the differentiation process generally goes relatively well. In this case, parents and young adults find a dynamic balance of connection and separation, of support and autonomy, and of mentoring without too much projection. Young adults define their identities and take ownership of their lives without cutting off contact from their parents and families. Parents remain involved in their children's lives, yet don't define their lives solely through their children. Both generations are able to utilize the process to define who they are, clarify their boundaries, and further their development rather than remaining stuck in developmentally inappropriate roles.

There are many thinkers who believe that, as a species, we are moving to higher levels of psychological and spiritual functioning. Among these is David Schnarch, author of "Passionate Marriage," who asserts that *differentiation is an evolutionary goal of the human species.* Specifically, the process of dealing with the differentiation dilemma, i.e., needing others and needing autonomy, is a primary vehicle through which we grow psychologically, intellectually, and emotionally. Being connected to others often provides some amount of security as well as some amount of emotional intrusiveness (others attempting to dictate to us or influence us). We can utilize the security as well as the intrusion to grow and further our differentiation. Both conditions are optimal for growth, and the balance between them is the key. The security of relationships provides a foundational springboard to take risks while emotional intrusions force us to define and clarify ourselves. In other words, the differentiation dilemma provides us with opportunities to define and assert ourselves *within* our relationships. The alternatives to healthy differentiation are being alienated from relationships or suffering the *soul crushing* consequences of allowing others to define who we are.

Characteristics of Well-Differentiated Individuals

Healthy differentiation is all about finding your own voice, your Real Self, within the context of relationships. It's about defining who you are without cutting off contact with others. Although differentiation levels can change based on context and circumstance, when the differentiation process goes well, individuals are able to attain high levels of psychological and relational health and exhibit a predictable set of characteristics, including the following.

Connection and Separation: Healthy Boundaries

When someone close to you is upset, do you feel responsible for making it better? Do you worry excessively about others' safety or feelings? Do you lose touch with who you are when you are in intimate relationships? Or, do you distance yourself when others get too close to you? Are you fiercely protective of your independence? Do you react strongly if you sense that others are becoming clingy or needy with you?

Poorly differentiated individuals tend to have difficulties with boundaries. If someone else is upset, they internalize that stress, which is a hallmark in fused relationships. Conversely, individuals with low levels of differentiation may avoid connections with others (i.e., they cut off from relationships) as a way of managing stress and the possibility of fusion.

Well-differentiated individuals, on the other hand, are able to connect to others without losing themselves. First and foremost, they can psychologically separate themselves from their parents without disengaging from them. They are able to find *emotional middle ground* between the extremes of fusion and cut off.

In addition to their parents, highly differentiated individuals have relationships with friends, intimate partners, and their own children that are characterized by emotional middle ground and *healthy boundaries*. Boundaries define where we end and where another begins, psychologically speaking. Boundaries regulate the amount of reactivity within relationships, with looser boundaries tending to lead to higher levels of reactivity.

Let me be clear that *boundaries are rarely defined solely by physical distance*, but by psychological perception and emotional experience. Individuals who have cut off from their parents, for example, are often distant physically but not psychologically. The distance is a reactive attempt to deal with unresolved fusion. In other words, the individual has not attained healthy levels of psychological separation; the distance is a pseudo attempt at differentiation. In these instances, individuals tend to reactively cut off from fused relationships with parents, and then enter into fused relationships with intimate peers.

Healthy boundaries, conversely, support intimate contact with others and a separate sense of self. Thus, healthy boundaries allow a person to be in close contact with other people without fears of being engulfed, overwhelmed, or eclipsed. A friend once remarked, "Healthy boundaries are like a gift you can give to another person; when you have healthy boundaries, the other person feels able to be close to you without fear that his/her personal space will be trampled." I strongly agree with this statement. Much of the subsequent discussion in this chapter will focus on the consequences of healthy and unhealthy interpersonal boundaries.

Low Levels of Emotional Reactivity

How quickly and easily do you become enraged, distraught, or experience strong emotions that feel overwhelming? How long does it take for you to return to a baseline level of emotional functioning after you have become emotionally upset? Do you feel like your life is an emotional roller coaster? When someone close to you is upset, do you react strongly to their emotions, maybe even stronger than they do? Do you tend to become defensive when you are given interpersonal feedback?

Emotional reactivity occurs when individuals respond to environmental stimuli with emotional flooding, emotional lability, or hypersensitivity. In other words, they become so activated by external stimuli that they become overwhelmed. To cope with this, they react in ways that are excessive and based more on the external stimuli than on their internal awareness. They lose touch with their Real Self and move into an externally reactive mode. One example would be reacting strongly to stimuli on television, such as a political figure. A person could be sitting calmly one moment, and then when a despised political figure appears on the television, the person instantly begins yelling profanities. The person is now in an emotionally reactive state.

Although reactivity largely depends on specific stimuli and contexts, such as yelling during a sporting event, some people exhibit greater levels of reactivity across a variety of contexts than do others. Some people are more susceptible to being overwhelmed by external stimuli, especially others' anxiety, and thus react more strongly. The primary root of high levels of emotional reactivity is poor boundaries. When individuals have poor boundaries, they become easily activated by external stimuli and can't easily regulate their emotional response. Thus, reactivity tends to lead to interpersonal defensiveness. Reactive individuals become quickly activated and feel the need to defend their positions or "correct" others. Other people often feel as if they are waking on eggshells when interacting with reactive individuals, making healthy communication difficult.

Highly differentiated individuals, however, have appropriate boundaries and therefore do not become as easily activated. This allows them to be in close proximity to external stimuli, such as another person's emotional state, without becoming overwhelmed. They can be near another person's anxiety and pain, for example, without claiming it as their own. They can hear feedback without becoming defensive. *They can be fully present with others without losing themselves.* This is a vital characteristic to have for effective psychotherapists, although it also comes in handy for all people because this balance is an essential aspect of most healthy intimate relationships.

Balanced Ownership of Responsibility

Do you believe that you can control another person's mood? Can you stop someone from drinking or using drugs? Can you make someone approve of you? Can you change the behavior of significant people in your life, like parents, siblings, spouse/partner, or children? Or, do you feel powerless to change the circumstances of your life?

Most people under- or over-estimate their ability to affect their world and relationships. Many believe that their happiness depends upon another person changing. In general, we suffer if we perceive we have no ability to change our lives. We also suffer if we continuously to try to change others or control our world. Differentiated people, by contrast, are more able to find a healthy balance between these two extremes. The healthy boundaries associated with high levels of differentiation allow individuals to know the limits of their responsibility and control.

I often say to clients that there are two ways for change to occur: love and duress. Loving relationships provide a secure base which allows us to experience intimacy, care, and strong attachments. As I have already alluded to, this foundation provides a springboard for risk-taking and growth. Relationships also typically provide some amount of emotional coercion and duress. Others are commenting on us and attempting to influence our thoughts and choices. Differentiating and successfully changing under duress commonly proceeds through a three-step process.

1. People point at a dynamic in their life that they don't like and say, "No, I don't want *that* anymore!"

2. They turn their finger from pointing externally back toward themselves and say, "*I* don't want to *do that* anymore."

3. They have the courage to make changes and act on their convictions.

In the first step, we become aware of a dynamic that is not working for us. It is important to objectify and label the dynamic so we know what we are addressing, so we see it when it emerges in our lives. The difference between step one and two is startling for most people. When we point our finger back toward ourselves, we move from a disempowered victim place, to a place of ownership and personal power. We more clearly see our role in the dynamics in our life. We become empowered.

Unfortunately, most people stop at the first step. They get so close to change, then back off and return to the same old patterns, because they are hoping that others will change. Instead of pointing at themselves, they point at others and demand that they change. Or, they start to own their values and lives, but fearfully choose not to act on their convictions. Either way, they return to a state of disempowerment.

I am not saying, like some will tell you, that we are responsible for everything that happens to us, such as being a victim of abuse. It is not your fault if you were abused; the abuser needs to be responsible for his/her actions and choices. What I am saying is when we define what isn't working in our lives, the power primarily rests with our ability to choose how we act, not waiting for another to change.

Well-differentiated individuals are more able to find the balance of what they are and are not responsible for in their lives. They realize how they act matters. They have power to affect their own as well as others' lives while also realizing their ability to change others is quite limited. As a psychotherapist, I deal with this paradox everyday. I am in the business of helping people change, yet I have very little control over their actual choices. I care deeply about my clients, yet they, not I, must act on their convictions and live with the consequences of their choices. I often say, "People are ornery." Thankfully, most people don't do what others want them to do or allow others to define them, at least not for long. Everyone must eventually take responsibility for his/her own life and choices.

Balance of Thoughts and Emotions

Do you feel overwhelmed by your emotions during stressful experiences? Does your sound judgment become impaired when you are emotional? Or, have people commented that you seem distant from your emotions? Do you feel safer when your emotions are under control?

Individuals who have struggled with the differentiation process tend to internalize the stress around them, which leads to excessive emotionality and dysregulation. Their emotions overwhelm their rational thought processes. They become prone to impulsive, reactive decisions. Other individuals have learned to cope with anxiety by distancing from their emotions, being excessively stoic. They become alienated from the emotional aspects of themselves and tend to project their denied emotions onto their partner.

Commonly, stoic and emotional types find each other and form a collusive partnership. They are drawn to the other person, who displays what they believe they don't have. Each plays out the denied parts of the other, sometimes in extreme fashion. Then they try to change their partner to be more like them, which, of course, creates a great deal of frustration for both. Their styles are flip sides of the same undifferentiated coin.

The extremes of excessive emotionality and stoicism mirror the relational patterns of fusion and cut off. Thus, both positions are associated with low levels of differentiation. Individuals with higher amounts of differentiation, by contrast, are able to separate thoughts from emotions. They have the ability to experience strong emotions without being flooded or overwhelmed by those emotions. They feel deeply, but don't lose their ability to think rationally. Individuals with high levels of differentiation, then, have the ability to experience strong affect as well as to shift into calm, logical reasoning when circumstances dictate.

Inner-Generated Convictions

How do you typically decide on a course of action in your life? What are the markers you use to assess if a course of action will be beneficial or not? What are your core values? How did you come to develop and know your values and beliefs? Are your beliefs truly your own or are your decisions based on your perception of how others will judge you?

Rick Johnson Ph.D.

Although we all have access to our Real Self, when we struggle with the differentiation process, we tend to be externally focused and reactive. We make decisions based on our perceptions of others' judgment of our decisions rather than on the inner wisdom of our Real Self. We alternate between accepting and acting upon what we think will gain approval and reactively pushing against our need for approval by actively choosing behaviors that will bring disapproval. This is what one client referred to as the "rebel without a cause" part of his personality. Either way, the development of our Real Self becomes inhibited.

Individuals with high levels of differentiation have an *inner-compass* that guides them in their lives and their decision-making, what in the differentiation literature is called a strong *I Position*. Of course, this inner compass is our Real Self. Through a healthy differentiation process, our Real Self is developed and emerges into awareness. We engage in an experiential search process that defines who we are: our values, beliefs, vocations, joys, passions, dislikes, and what makes our soul sing. We do not blindly accept the identity markers that others preach, nor do we reject them reactively. We take in the wisdom of others as well as experience life for ourselves. Through the differentiation process we find our voice and connect to the wisdom of our Real Self.

Ability to Self-Soothe

What do you do when you are emotionally distraught or *dysregulated*? How do you calm yourself down? Do you externalize the anguish by blaming others? Do you turn your pain back onto yourself, either emotionally or physically? Do you shut down your emotions? Do you engage in behaviors that end up bringing you more pain? How long does it take to regain a sense of calm? How long before you become distraught again?

The differentiation process is about learning to tolerate the fear and frustration associated with developing autonomy and mastery in the world. When it goes well, the process begins with a secure bond between child and parent, which allows children to imagine a caring and supportive parent even when that parent is not physically present. This ability to borrow ego strength from a parent sets the stage for the development of self-soothing skills. As the differentiation process continues, a clear sense of self emerges, including confidence in one's abilities to manage the anxieties of life.

Individuals with low levels of differentiation lack self-soothing skills and, therefore, have difficulty experiencing intense emotions without becoming flooded or shutting down. They utilize a variety of strategies to compensate for this difficulty, including internalizing and externalizing blame. Internalizers attempt to regain some sense of inner calm by blaming or hurting themselves. Externalizers attempt to regain inner calm by blaming, hurting, or focusing on others. Either way, they become activated by anxiety and reactive. They lack the ability to tolerate anxiety and various uncomfortable emotions without engaging in behaviors that are costly to their psychological and relational health.

Although we all become activated by stress and anxiety, well-differentiated individuals are able to maintain their sense of self in the face of anxiety. They are able to self-soothe. They exhibit the ability to experience their emotions without shutting down or acting out, on others or themselves. Even when anxious, they experience their emotions and then are able to return to a centered sense of self. They rarely lose touch with their Real Self for long.

Rick Johnson Ph.D.

Direct Communication

What do you do when someone upsets you, like your parent, spouse/partner, friend, or boss? Do you speak to that person directly? Or, do you talk to others about that person? Do you tell your kids, if you have them, when your spouse/partner hurts your feelings? What is the purpose of telling others: sympathy, venting, a coalition against the person, or advice as to how to proceed?

The reactivity and poor boundaries associated with individuals who have struggled with the differentiation process make direct communication less likely. In general, their relationships are characterized by high levels of drama. Fusion, by nature, lacks psychological separateness and leads to reactivity and interpersonal drama. Fusion invariably requires the inclusion of a third person into relational dynamics. In other words, poorly differentiated individuals lack the ability to handle interpersonal stress without venting that stress and attempting to stabilize their relationships by including others in their relational dynamics.

Similarly, when individuals haven't been able to define who they are or deal with fusion without reactively cutting off, they tend to struggle with this throughout their lives. They tend to shut down or include others in their relationships, especially when anxiety increases. If they were recipients of parental projection in childhood, especially *triangulation*, they tend to repeat the same patterns in adulthood and with their own children and intimate partners. They tend to include their children in their marital conflicts, which makes it difficult for their children to get close to one parent without the other parent being threatened.

Well-differentiated individuals, with their healthy boundaries and low levels of reactivity, rarely engage in gossip and triangulation. They can tolerate others' pain and relational anxiety without becoming reactive and threatened. They don't need to involve others or shut down. They have the confidence to deal with their relationships directly and the ability to self-soothe without triangulating others in their interpersonal dynamics. They realize that, in most cases, it is far more effective to deal directly with someone than it is to complain and attempt to get others on their side.

Adult-to-Adult Relationships with Parents

Are you afraid of your parents? Do you find yourself acting in developmentally inappropriate ways when you are around your parents? Are you able to express yourself freely with your parents, including when you are unhappy with them? What is your level of acceptance of your parents? If your parents are deceased, were you able to achieve a level of comfort and acceptance with yourself and them before they died?

For many of us, the first 20 or so years of life are about finding our way within a particular family system. Parents are very large figures that dominate our life and decision-making. Parents seem bigger than life. As we age, we define and assert ourselves; however, many people never achieve a sense of personal power in relation to their parents. They continue to see *their parents through child's eyes.*

Part of the differentiation process is coming to terms with the good news and bad news about your parents and your family of origin. Each family has its strengths and weaknesses. In most cases, parents do as well as they can considering their upbringing and life circumstances. Each new generation has the ability to become aware of the consequences of growing up in a particular family situation. This awareness can be translated into higher levels of differentiation than the previous generation, through

Rick Johnson Ph.D.

ownership of one's life. Eventually, we need to understand the ways our families have shaped our lives, then transcend those familiar patterns and roles and connect with our own wisdom, vision, and personal power.

The degree to which individuals are able to view their parents as equals tends to be contingent upon cultural factors. Some cultures do not have a conceptual framework for this that wouldn't be considered disrespectful. However, as they evolve psychologically, most people are able to eventually understand the basic humanity of their parents. When this happens, we no longer cower in relation to our parents or attribute omnipotent characteristics to them. As we own our personal power and inner-generated sense of self, we begin to relate to our parents with a shared and compassionate understanding of the existential dilemmas of living. Parents are travelers, as we all are, trying to create meaning, find their way, and deal with the uncertainties of living life and the certainty of facing death. Healthy differentiation allows us to see our parents through compassionate and accepting eyes as we more fully take responsibility for our life. Differentiation allows us to truly *choose* to be with our parents, sharing time and experiences, rather than acting out of obligation or powerlessness.

Personal Authority

Do you feel confident and efficacious in your life? Do you believe that you have personal rights? Do you feel responsible for your own life? Do you have confidence in your ability to be intimate with others while establishing clear personal boundaries? Or, are you afraid to be assertive with others for fear of being rejected or abandoned? Do you believe you need other people to take responsibility for you, which negates your rights or personal

122

power?

Personal authority relates to the belief that we have the right and ability to meet our needs. It is a sense of personal efficacy. Many people refer to it as *personal power*. It isn't power to control, dominate or manipulate others. It is power in your own life. At its core, personal authority is about taking responsibility for your own life and choices.

When the differentiation process goes poorly, individuals are busy reacting to others, be it to please or to rebel. They lose touch with their inner compass. Their relational consciousness is caught up with controlling others or reacting to being controlled by others. Either position is undifferentiated and alienated from the Real Self. Tying your self-worth to your ability to change another person is unwise and precarious; your personal power is not yours. Conversely, allowing others to control you is equally soul-crushing. Either way, your personal power lies outside of your consciousness and you suffer.

Well-differentiated individuals have a strong sense of personal authority. They do not need others to take responsibility for their lives. And, they freely *choose* to be in relationships, not out of obligation or fear. They know they have the ability to get their needs met across many areas in their life. They know who they are and are not afraid to embrace their personal power. This sense of efficacy in the world is the culmination of the differentiation process, which has supported life-learning and ownership for one's choices. A healthy differentiation process leads to clarity about what is life-affirming and confidence and courage to act on those convictions.

Rick Johnson Ph.D.

Personal Integrity

Do you have a vision for what is meaningful in your life? On what have you based this vision? How often do you have an inner knowing about what is right for you? Do you let it guide your life and decision-making? Or, do you ignore its wisdom? What are the organizing themes or principles in your life? Are these themes life-affirming?

Poorly differentiated individuals have difficulty answering these questions. They often do not know what is meaningful to them. They do not have a consistent sense of the organizing themes in their life. Or, the themes seem superficial and based on interpersonal drama rather than based on personal ownership. Their sense of personal consciousness is largely externally based. They are busy playing roles that have been prescribed to them or they are reacting against these roles. Their lives are not their own. They lack connection to an inner compass.

Individuals with high levels of differentiation have all the ingredients for a strong, life-affirming sense of personal integrity. The differentiation process has forged inner-generated convictions. These convictions have developed from a balanced place of connection with others and healthy boundaries. Well-differentiated individuals are not simply reacting to others, but are proactive in their beliefs and choices. They experience the emotionality of life without losing touch with their rational thought processes. They have the ability to self-soothe and manage the anxieties inherent in living. All of which has forged a strong sense of confidence in their beliefs and abilities. Thus, their behaviors and choices are congruent with their inner-generated convictions.

When we act in ways that are in accordance with our values and core beliefs, we act from our personal integrity. As Schnarch says, we courageously *hold onto ourselves*, even risking disapproval and rejection from others. The opinions and approval of others may change, but our personal integrity will be our consistent guidepost. *Our personal integrity represents the consciousness of our Real Self.*

Increasing Differentiation

Differentiation is a developmental process, but can also be intentional. As children, we have a limited view of normalcy. We assume, no matter how crazy our families may be, that they are normal. We have very limited reference points against which to judge our experiences. We mostly just react to the psychological energies and emotional entanglements of our families of origin. Our developmental needs and capabilities interact with the emotional and psychological climate of our family context. Thus, our attempts to define ourselves are mostly reactive rather than intentional.

As we age, we see more examples of different kinds of families and family interactions and our view of normal expands. We develop a more consistent ability to reflect on and define relationship dynamics, rather than just react to them. As teenagers, we typically categorize and objectify our parents, but we don't yet possess the emotional maturity or psychological distance to understand them as real people. We tend to see them as caricatures, which is a way to deal with the psychological intrusion that parents represent to us.

It isn't until we physically leave home that we typically begin to have enough emotional distance from our parents to begin to define who we are in relation to our families in intentional and proactive ways. This tends to be a slow process, with many opportunities to define who we are or suffer the consequences of not doing so. Differentiation, then, is not an event that happens just once, although profound opportunities and defining moments may occur periodically. The process of increasing differentiation is more like an unfolding of awareness, which provides opportunities to seize ownership of one's life. Thus, the process of consciously and intentionally increasing differentiation occurs for most people as adults, if at all.

The original thinking about the ability to increase differentiation, in fact, was quite pessimistic. The belief was that we are about as differentiated as our parents, and without considerable effort and therapy, raising our level was not often achieved. Most contemporary differentiation theorists, however, are more optimistic about our chances of intentionally increasing our psychological health. Along with the developmental trajectory of our lives, intentionally increasing differentiation tends to involve two continually repeating steps of awareness and ownership.

Awareness

How do you become aware of your differentiation level? A helpful place to start is by increasing your awareness of your emotional, psychological, and functional place in your family of origin. What roles did you play in your family? How reactive were your attempts at self-definition? Are you playing the same roles and acting out the same strategies with them now? Have you continued these roles and dynamics in your current friendships and intimate relationships?

Once you begin to grasp the key markers of differentiation, it is often useful to interact with your family while consciously considering these ideas and characteristics. When you attend family functions, for example, consciously observe yourself and your family. What roles do you and other members take? Are their spoken or unspoken rules that dictate the dynamics and proceedings? What happens if you don't play your typical role or follow the rules? Do you feel a pull from others for you to play your role or intervene in certain relational dynamics?

The goal at this phase is to simply increase your awareness of the rules, roles, and beliefs that typically operate in your family. You can then look at how these themes and relational dynamics may be operating in other aspects of your life: friends, coworkers, intimate partners, etc. All of your relationships provide opportunities to observe and learn about your level of psychological health. Increasing your awareness provides you with the ability to choose how you want to conduct yourself. Choice then leads to the ability to increase your ownership across all your relationships and life-decisions.

Ownership

Ownership means taking responsibility for your life, not just blindly repeating patterns. Once you increase your awareness of your relational dynamics, you have more ability to choose how you act. You can choose to play or not play certain roles in your life.

For example, if you become aware that you tend to be a caretaker of others and that you negate your own needs while accommodating others, you may decide that it is time to selectively set boundaries, to say "no" to other people at times, and to say "yes" to your own needs. This will likely activate a pull-back response from others; they are used to you being a certain way and playing a certain role in their life. They will expect the status quo and want you to return to your unspoken role. Awareness and ownership provide you with the ability to decide how you want to respond to these pulls. It is your life—you must live with the consequences of your choices.

A common misperception is that taking ownership for

your life means that you will become self-centered, that you will neglect the needs of others because you are focusing on your own. Although this notion tends to have some truth initially, it misses the true nature of ownership. Individuals who have just started increasing their awareness and ownership are not practiced at doing so. They tend to be more self-focused and to emphasize boundaries because they are realizing how often they allowed them to be crossed in the past. This process is a developmental one, and tends to become less reactive with practice.

True ownership is about living a *value-driven life*—living your life based on your own values, which have been forged through life experience, not by blindly accepting what has been imposed on you. Your values will likely include forming and maintaining relationships as well as engaging in more individual pursuits. Sustainable ownership requires that you intentionally choose and balance all your values and needs. In other words, increasing your differentiation requires you to become aware of your patterns, and then to choose how you meet and balance your needs for connection and autonomy.

As I have said, this process leads to the development of your personal integrity, which is the voice and consciousness of your Real Self. Personal integrity is one of the many aspects of healthy psychological function that can be supported through the inclusion of spiritual practice. Awakening to and embracing Spiritual Energy nourishes your Real Self. In the next chapter, I will discuss how spiritual practice can support the development of your personal integrity and health.

Chapter 7
Spiritual Health and Abundance: Practical Steps

"To discover an inner power that is completely good and gentle is frightening; it robs us of every comfort, every safety in resignation or irony. Who can live naked to his own perfection? And yet who, once seeing and acknowledging his own perfection, could bear not to try to realize it in living?"

Thuksey Rinpoche, cited in Andrew Harvey's
A Journey in Ladakh

There are many ways that spirituality can inform and support healthy living. Most notably, spiritual practice can be a central aspect in developing personal integrity and a guide in defining and achieving health and growth. There are several key steps involved in the process of spiritual nourishment, especially as an adjunct to a psychotherapeutic approach. These are: (a) awakening to spirituality, (b) cultivating personal integrity, (c) evaluating life-structures, and (d) remembering and committing to spiritual practice.

Awakening to Spirituality

The first step in utilizing Spiritual Energy to further personal growth is to ask yourself the question: *What is my personal definition of spirituality?* Spirituality is a very personal issue. Each of us needs to come to our own ways of defining, experiencing,

Rick Johnson Ph.D.

and expressing a philosophical and spiritual grounding. The following questions can assist you in the process of understanding your spirituality:

- What was I taught as a child about spirituality?
- Which, if any, of the definitions and values of spirituality that I was taught as a child fit for me today?
- Is there a distinction for me between organized religion and spirituality?
- When in my life have I felt a *life-affirming* sense of spirituality?
- What rituals or activities support my spirituality?
- How does a life-affirming sense of spirituality emerge now in my life?

Think outside the box—spirituality may emerge in nontraditional ways such as artistic expression, nature, stillness, awareness of your breath, movement, relationships or encounters, images or symbols, physical sensations, coincidences, intuition, feelings of being in-flow, moments of clarity and interconnection, and connections to your heart and heart-based experience. If you don't typically categorize these types of experiences as spiritual, it may be a shift for you to do so. Of course, your sense of spirituality may be mostly associated with organized religion and more traditional practices such as prayer. I believe it is not important where or how Spiritual Energy is accessed. What matters most is if the avenue of experiencing spirituality is life-affirming. Does the spiritual practice evoke feelings of love, peace, and clarity? Does it warm and nourish your heart? Does it help you take perspective in ways that reduce fear and increase a sense of your connection in the world?

The phrase that most facilitated my spiritual journey as a young adult was: *Be open to the possibilities.* Before slowly adopting this phrase and the associated openness, I had been on a multiyear path of intellectual nihilism. I was focused on rebutting theories I saw as fake or unsubstantiated. I prided myself on knocking holes in faith-based arguments related to the existence of God, for example. If it couldn't be empirically tested, then it didn't exist. I perceived much of society and associated life structures as contrived, superficial, and lacking substance and meaning. Unfortunately, my excessive rationalism alienated me from others and from affective and "non-rational" ways of knowing. During this period, I was quite alienated from the intuitive knowing of my Real Self. I was often depressed, lonely, and angry.

Being open to possibilities started for me as a mental shift, a shift in consciousness. If I was open to the possibilities of experience beyond rationalism, what might emerge? What started to emerge for me, as it does for many people, was a sense that there is more to life than meets the eye.

First, I started to notice interesting coincidences that seemed to defy logic. It seemed as though people would come into my life, sometimes only very briefly, with information or messages I needed to hear. If I was open and ready to receive the message, my life and learning were propelled in some way; and I could provide others with energy or experiences that seemed to assist them in their journey. It felt like some guidance or external energy was part of what was happening. I have heard numerous people describe these types of experiences as "God whispering in your ear." It is also what Jung referred to as *synchronicity*.

These experiences generated a series of questions for me. Why were these coincidences occurring? Was there some intelligence behind these occurrences? Was this revealing some interconnecting energy in the world? Although I couldn't (and still can't) provide scientifically-based answers to these and many other questions, powerful coincidences continued to occur as long as I was awake to the possibilities.

As I became more open to the possibilities, I also started to find clarity and guidance coming through intuitive channels. When I could quiet down my excessive rationalism and task-focused brain, my intuitive knowing began to increase. It was as if I had access to truths and clarity, such as sensing the interconnectedness of existence. I could *see* energy passing between people and among all things. I started to *talk* to trees and be grateful for their energy. I became more aware of my present moment experience. I started to have a more open and accepting perspective on suffering. My compassion for myself and others increased. I felt my heart begin to awaken.

For me these experiences felt like remembering something I already knew rather than new experiences. Somehow I was relearning rather than learning. And, again it felt as if it came from both internal and external sources, what I now refer to as *inner knowing and external presence.* When I was quiet and settled within myself and aware of my breath, I was most able to remember and connect with this intuitive knowing. I was most able to *hear God whispering in my ear.*

I began to notice that this inner knowing and external presence was possible to experience at all times, as though it was waiting to be accessed. All that was required was present moment awareness and an open heart. There also seemed to be interplay between potentialities and free will, that is: intuitive knowing and guidance were always available, but it was up to me to be awake and open. And, I still had the responsibility to choose any course of action based on intuitive knowledge.

The most important consequence of my being open to possibilities is that my life has improved tremendously. Acknowledging that I don't understand the totality of spirituality provides me with a great deal of comfort and relief. I don't think any of us has all the answers. As a matter of fact, an agnostic position may be the only truly tenable mindset. However, I believe that Spiritual Energy exists, even if I can't completely know or understand it. What I feel sure of is that when I remember to be in the present moment, I have access to perspective, intuitive knowing, and guidance that make my life better.

From these initial, powerful experiences I have learned to be open to various ways of connecting to Spiritual Energy, including many that are discussed in this book. The easiest and most reliable way for me to connect to Spiritual Energy is by being awake and aware in the present, what is often referred to as *mindfulness.* Again, it doesn't matter how you access spirituality, but whether your beliefs and practices are life-affirming. Spiritual Energy is available every moment; you need to simply *open yourself to the possibility.*

As a practicing psychologist, I regularly invite clients to consider their personal definitions of spirituality and how they access Spiritual Energy. I always begin by meeting clients exactly where they are with their current beliefs. Many people have had negative and judgment-filled experiences with organized religion; consequently, some are quite reactive to any conversation about spirituality. It is important to honor clients where they are and validate their experiences. For some it may be months before they talk in detail about their own beliefs about and experiences with spirituality.

Even when clients don't talk explicitly about spirituality, it still emerges in our discussions. I listen for what makes them feel alive, what makes their hearts sing. I listen for whatever is life-affirming for them, and then watch as it emerges in the therapy room: clarity, joy, perspective, wisdom, positive risk-taking, visions of health, ownership of a clear voice, and moments of authentic connection, to name a few.

Sometimes Spiritual Energy emerges in ways that are not typical. As an example, I had one client who was raised without much religious or spiritual guidance from her family. Her past experiences with organized religion were mostly negative. She was not interested in talking about spirituality. She had grown up with an alcoholic single mother and her greatest struggles were with feelings of being un-deserving of love and attention. One day she called late, with many apologies, and cancelled our session. At the next scheduled session I asked her what was happening that she had to cancel. She indicated that she had gone horseback riding, something she loved but hadn't given herself permission to do in many years. Her initial expectation was that I would be disappointed and critical that she cancelled. Instead, I eagerly listened and watched her face light up as she described how her "heart opened-up" while she was riding—like a "warm wind" blowing through her chest. She felt happy, peaceful, clear, and more confident than she had in recent memory. She spontaneously described it as a spiritual experience.

This event provided many gifts for her and her therapy. First, I was supportive of her horseback riding rather than being critical of her like her mother typically was. Her trust in me increased and it provided a corrective emotional experience in that she realized she deserved support from others and happiness. Most important, her "spiritual experience" was a grounding and defining experience: she could remember the feelings in her chest, use those feelings as a barometer of her own strength and wisdom, and could recreate those feelings, either mentally by remembering or physically by getting back on a horse. Those positive feelings were central to her knowing and striving for health, even as she processed difficult experiences in her past and current life.

Cultivating Personal Integrity

Once you are more open to the possibility of spirituality and both define and embrace your access to its personal presence in your life, the next step is to allow Spiritual Energy to inform your values and to shape your personal integrity. As I have discussed, the essence of personal integrity is living your life in accordance with what you know is right. Personal integrity is your inner, moral compass. It is about personal values, which have been forged through life experience. It is about answering to your inner-knowing, looking at yourself in the mirror. It's about owning your truth. Only when your actions are solidly aligned with your personal convictions do you achieve the sense of wholeness that defines integrity.

I have come to believe that we know what is right. Our Real Self provides this clarity and wisdom if we listen. The inner-knowing of our Real Self provides the substance of our personal integrity. As I said in the last chapter, *personal integrity represents the voice and consciousness of our Real Self.*

We oftentimes choose not to listen to this inner-knowledge, however. We make decisions based on our fears or misgivings rather than from our Real Self. We desperately want to be liked and accepted, so we trade in our inner-wisdom for the hope of attaining approval from others. Then we feel like we are living our life for other people, and ultimately we feel lost. We also can become so self-absorbed that we lose sight of the bigger picture. What really is lost is our connection to our personal integrity.

The good news is that our personal integrity does not have to be lost forever. It can always be re-claimed. We can learn to clarify our values and courageously assert these values through our choices and behaviors. We can live a *value-driven life*.

A value-driven life is about following your inner-generated beliefs and moral compass. It is not about doing what others want. Neither is it about doing what others don't want. It is about doing what you know is right. A value-driven life is about taking ownership for your life and choices. *No one else can make you happy.* Only you can take charge of your own life and happiness, including choosing partners and friends who will support your happiness. If you are waiting for others to change or for others to give you permission to change, you will suffer greatly. You must claim your own life. If your choices are based on the wisdom of your Real Self, it will be an expression of your personal integrity.

Some may argue that a value-driven life can be selfish, that we need to consider others' feelings and needs not just our own. I agree that we need to be sensitive to others, aware of how our behavior affects others, and to take responsibility for the consequences of our actions. When we listen to and follow our Real Self and personal integrity, we naturally make choices which are healthy and life-affirming for ourselves and others. We don't act in ways that are cruel, demeaning, or life-detracting to others. Despite fears to the contrary, when we follow our personal integrity we don't suddenly become lazy, selfish, or criminal in our actions. When our Real Self leads the way, our personal integrity includes a core value related to being compassionate and sensitive to others.

I often tell my clients to *partner with health.* Your Real Self will be your voice of health. Not everyone may like your choices. However, when you act from a mindset of health and ownership for your life rather than fear and attempting to please others, you will naturally make life-affirming decisions.

So, how do you know what is right? How do you know what is healthy? How do you cultivate your personal integrity and partner with health?

Any personal growth process, like psychotherapy or a spiritual practice, which helps clarify your values and increase ownership for your identity and choices, can help you live a value-driven life. The key is that the process should be about supporting the development of your own core values rather than imposing a belief system. Spiritual Energy, in particular, can inform and guide this process if you open your heart. The most important step is to become quiet enough to listen. You have to quiet the external noise related to how others try to define your life. You also have to quiet your internal fears and self-deprecating thoughts. Your decisions will not be successful or sustainable if they are not your own or if they are based on fear. They must be based on your inner knowing, which can be enhanced by opening your heart and being receptive to the Spiritual Energy that is available to you. Let your spiritual practice clarify your values, support your intuition, and guide your life. Let your actions in day-to-day life as well as your major life decisions be informed from your spiritual center. Like my client, conduct your life based on the state of mind that is achieved when *riding your horse*. Then, you will be living a spiritual, value-driven life that represents what is truest and best about your innermost being.

Evaluating Life Structures

When we live a value-driven life, we become discerning of experiences. We awaken our senses to what is life-detracting and what is life-affirming, to what supports or detracts from our health. We naturally start to value what is life-affirming and limit what is not. We begin to *define and live health.*

As I have said, I often help clients to define and partner with health. I regularly ask them to consider what they have learned thus far in their lives about what works for them, what brings meaning to their lives. When I first direct them to consider health, they typically are so busy battling dysfunction and dealing with pain they can't easily do it. They have become lost and have forgotten to embrace what is good and life-affirming for them.

I conceptualize health as activities and experiences that we know on an intuitive and heart-based level are affirming and meaningful for us. In fact, most often what constitutes health is what is meaningful. Meaning is what makes getting out of bed each morning truly possible. Life can't be just about various kinds of attainment, such as status or possessions. Life also can't be defined by the avoidance of what scares us. When we stop chasing happiness through attainment of material possessions or running away in fear, we find meaning.

The essence of a meaningful life is allowing your personal integrity and Real Self to evaluate your choices and dictate your life path. If you are similar to most people, you need to give your life a good shaking, like shaking the dust out of a throw rug. The cream of your life, seen through the eyes of your Real Self, will rise to the top of your consciousness and life-detracting experiences will feel empty, lifeless, and painful. Life-detracting experiences create a sense of incongruency and anxiety. When you are not living in accordance with the wisdom of your Real Self, you will experience a sense that you are not *fully inhabiting* your life. Parts of you are excluded, removed from awareness, or blocked.

I think of life structures as the activities, relationships, and experiences that comprise your life. These can be categorized into six foundational areas: (a) physical, (b) relationships, (c) work and leisure activities, (d) financial, (e) community, and (f) spiritual/ philosophical. Right now, consider your life across each of these areas. Are you embracing health and what is life-affirming or are you spinning your wheels and missing the mark?

Physical

How well are you caring for your body and supporting your physical health? What kind of exercise do you get—is it right for your body? How well do you identify and manage stress? Are you *in touch* with your emotions and your body? Do you eat when you are hungry? Or, do you become so task-focused that you forget to eat? Do you have some amounts of chronic or periodic pain: back or neck pain, headaches, stomach discomfort, etc.? Do you ignore your body, only to experience intense discomfort occasionally? If you have physical ailments or pain, are your lifestyle choices exacerbating or healing your condition?

Physical health is about how well you care for your physical self, such as eating, sleeping, getting exercise, managing stress, and listening to your body. It is about understanding and re-specting the natural rhythms of your being. Your body will tell you much about what it needs—when you are hungry or tired, for example. Your body can also tell you which forms of exercise are best for you, and what kinds of food and nutrients you need. The key is to listen. Many people are so busy following routines and completing externally-based tasks that they forget to reflect internally. Each of the activities associated with your physical self can be evaluated to see if they are life-affirming, and altered if need be.

Rick Johnson Ph.D.

Relationships

To what degree do your relationships support your health and nourish your being? Do you feel controlled by others? Do you feel like you need to be different to please others? Do you feel your energy being drained or replenished in your relationships? Do you have a need to change or control others? Do you like who you are in your relationships? Are you satisfied with the level of depth and meaning versus superficiality in your relationships? To what degree are you fully present in your relationships? To what degree do you trust that your significant others will be there for you if you need help or comfort?

Relationships include intimate partners, children, parents, extended family, friends, co-workers, and to a lesser degree, causal acquaintances. One of the most foundational human needs is social connection. The need is so strong that many people desperately hold onto life-detracting relationships rather than face the terrifying possibility of being alone. For most of us, the quality of our primary relationships is the strongest predictor of our sense of well-being. The more that are relationships are life-affirming, the better we tend to feel about ourselves and our lives. If the attachment and security of our primary relationships are compromised or fragile, we feel anxious, unsatisfied, incomplete, and untethered. Being seen, understood, accepted, and loved within significant relationships lead to a sense of meaning, purpose, self-esteem, and grounding in the world. Without life-affirming relationships we experience the world as orphans; we feel alone and lost.

Work and Leisure

Do you derive meaning and passion from your work and leisure activities? Is your work "just a job" or is it a calling? Do you dread going to work and have to drag yourself out of bed in the morning? Conversely, do you overwork? Do you use work as an escape from other areas of your life? Do your leisure activities reflect your passions and core values? Are you satisfied with your balance between work and leisure activities?

This category includes paid work, volunteering, avocations, and leisure activities. Freud argued that love and work are the two essential ingredients for a meaningful life. I think this is largely true. Almost all of the clients that come into my clinical practice have issues with their primary relationships; most struggle with both relationships and work. For most of us, work takes up the largest portion of our day-to-day lives. If it is not satisfying and meaningful, then we are spending the majority of our waking hours engaged in an activity which is not life-affirming. Our consciousness is filled with and reminded of what is lacking and unsatisfying. We often will feel listless and bored. By contrast, when our work and activities are meaningful and congruent with our core values, we feel alive and purposeful.

Financial

How do you view money? What feelings does it evoke in you—fear, joy, guilt, envy, inadequacy, dispassionate interest, etc.? What role does money have in your day-to-day life? How much of your consciousness is filled with thoughts about money—not having enough, ways to make more, etc.? How well do you manage your money? Does your money work for you or do you work for your money?

The importance of reaching a place of peace and perspective related to finances can't be overstated. Much suffering in the world occurs due to money, most often related to feeling a sense of insecurity and lack. People will engage in morally reprehensible behavior when they don't have enough money to meet their basic needs. Even after basic needs are met, some people will take great risks and compromise their personal integrity in an attempt to obtain more money. People often are afraid of not having enough, long after they have plenty of money. Sometimes the more money people have the less generous they become.

Money is something that should enhance your life rather than detract from it. Many of us work so hard to earn more money that we don't have enough time and energy to enjoy it. Shifts in perspective occur when we think about money as a means to enhance life, align with and be an expression of core values, and support life-affirming activities. Money can provide security as well as options and choices. A sound financial foundation coupled with a healthy perspective on money provides the freedom to engage in soul-nourishing activities as well as freedom from the perpetual search for more and more.

Community

What are the primary social groups or organizations in which you function (e.g., schools, work, and community)? Do you like and respect the social organizations and community in which you live? To what degree do you identify yourself as being part of your community? Do you feel as if you belong there? Have you found a life-affirming, meaningful, and helpful place in your social structures? Or, do you feel like you are *just a visitor* in these structures?

This category deals with our sense of self vis-à-vis our social groups and larger community. Alfred Adler, a contemporary of Freud, posited that happiness and success in life are largely a function of social connectedness and finding a niche within our primary social organizations, such as schools, work places, and communities. When we lack a sense of connection with and useful place within our social structures, we are likely to become isolated and discouraged. By contrast, when take an active interest in the welfare of others within our community, what Adler termed *social interest*, we feel purposeful and positively connected to larger social goals. Research has provided support to Adler's assertions, identifying social connectedness and a sense of social interest as predictors of psychological adjustment and health in children and adults.

Spiritual/Philosophical

What are your beliefs about the meaning and purpose of your life? To what degree are your spiritual beliefs and practices life-affirming? To what degree are your spiritual beliefs and practices based on love and abundance versus fear and scarcity? How do your spiritual beliefs and practices influence your behaviors and thoughts toward others? How much time do you spend reflecting on spiritual and philosophical questions? Do you avoid these types of questions about meaning and spiritual/philosophical worldviews?

This category deals with the ways in which we make sense of our existence. We all have some ideas and practices related to beliefs about existence, including agnostic and atheistic positions. Different spiritual and philosophical beliefs can have radically different outcomes related to how we think about ourselves in the world. For example, there are vast differences in beliefs about the degree to which life is governed by chance and randomness versus an intentional and purposeful force. Each conceptual position has ramifications related to the degree to which we embrace ideas of free will and order in our lives. What matters most, in my view, is not the content of the beliefs, but the degree to which the beliefs are life-affirming. Generally speaking, spiritual views and practices that enhance feelings of love and compassion for self and others are more life-affirming while those that promote fear through a restrictive, moralistic vision tend to be more life-detracting.

An evaluation of life structures can be painful and reveal areas where you are not embracing health. Realizing that certain life structures are not supporting your health can lead to difficult questions and decisions. For example,

- To what degree are problematic life structures incompatible with your personal integrity and vision of health?
- What keeps you holding onto life-detracting activities, relationships or practices?
- What role is fear playing in your choice to maintain certain life structures?
- Can shifts occur to bring problematic life structures in-line with your personal integrity and vision of health?
- Do you need to remove or reduce your participation in certain life structures or increase participation in others?

An important part of this evaluation process is to not *pathologize the underlying needs* across all these areas of your life. The needs associated with meaningful work, satisfying intimate relationships, financial security, social connectedness, and existential beliefs are not problematic; they are simply part of life. What is assessed closely is how you are trying are meet these needs. Are the ways that you are attempting to meet your needs life-affirming and congruent with your core values? It doesn't work to try to eliminate your needs; the focus is on evaluating and modifying the methods and structures associated with meeting your needs.

This assessment process can be particularly difficult when your relationships are the focus. In this case, I encourage you to embrace your personal vision of health and *invite others to join you in health*. In other words, come from a place of personal integrity and ask others to respond to you on that level. Invite them to meet you and support your attempts to practice health in your life. If others won't take the invitation and, instead, consistently try to restrict your health and what is life-affirming for you, the relationship itself will need to re-assessed. As a general and simplified rule of thumb, embrace relationships and activities that are life-affirming and limit those that are life-detracting. Although it sounds simple, many people choose to continue with life-detracting relationships and activities rather than deal with the fear and upheaval of major change.

Psychotherapy can be a vital resource to assist with the evaluation process and the implementation of changes. Therapy can help you clarify your values and deepen your connection with your Real Self as well as provide support of courageous decision-making. Therapy can also assist your significant others by increasing their understanding and support for your life changes. A fear-based and controlling husband, for example, can be supported and challenged in marital therapy related to his fears and thoughts about his wife's changes. It may be possible for him to embrace her health rather than be threatened by the changes. If he can support her health, he can join her on the path. If not, they may need to make changes in the nature of their relationship.

Rick Johnson Ph.D.

Remembering and Committing to Spiritual Practice

Spiritual Energy is available every moment. We simply have to remember to invite it into our lives and hearts and to engage in spiritual practice that will invoke its power. As I have said, most people experience spiritual truths as confirmatory rather than new information. Thus, we just need to remember what we already know.

Life-affirming spiritual practice will provide us with a vehicle through which we can remember and experience Spiritual Energy. Unfortunately, it is very easy to become reactively engaged in life and forget what truly matters. You may have a deeply spiritual experience one day, and then quickly return to your familiar ways of engaging in the world the next, only to have another discreet experience that reminds you of what is available. This is why it is called *practice*. We must practice regularly to become experts on our own spiritual lives. We must be committed to a practice that reminds us to be awake to Spiritual Energy.

There are many ways to engage in spiritual practice. What matters most is if the practice is life-affirming and *that* you do it, not *how* you do it. Engage in your spiritual practice through regularly scheduled activities as well as every moment through mindful awareness. *Be open to the possibility of Spiritual Energy* and practice whatever works for you. So, go horseback riding, go hiking, meditate, pray, go to church, do yoga, breathe, smile, enjoy the arts, connect to others with compassion and acceptance, and be mindful in your moment by moment activities. Be awake to the Holy Spirit as it emerges through all things. Embrace God's life breath; it is in you and everything around you. All that is needed is for you to remember its presence and be open to the possibilities that naturally emerge.

Chapter 8
Integrating your Shadow

"If it is important for me to live a pure life, I must be preoccupied with impurity: I must discriminate all situations and my responses to them into pure and impure. To bifurcate in this way is also to bifurcate myself from the situation; being *pure* in a situation becomes more important than *living* that situation."

David Loy, *Lack and Transcendence*

The last chapter focused on how Spiritual Energy and a life-affirming spiritual practice can inform, support, and nourish the development of our personal integrity. The activities and relationships that make up our lives can then be evaluated based on the vision and standards of our personal integrity. In this way our personal integrity becomes our moral barometer and guiding voice in our lives. As desirable as this is, if our moral code becomes restrictive and legalistic, a variety of psychological and spiritual problems can develop, including disconnection from our Real Self and other aspects of our consciousness. Our conscious understanding of ourselves becomes increasingly limited in the face of restrictive moral standards. We deem some of our needs and parts of our consciousness as unacceptable, thus fostering the development of a *shadow* part of our personality—those parts of ourselves we have difficulty acknowledging and incorporating.

By remaining unaware of our shadow, we feel safe from anxiety in the short-term, but do so at great peril in the longer-term. We are likely to act out our shadow-needs in ways which contradict our personal integrity, causing harm to ourselves and others. A sustainable moral vision needs to include all of who we are. All of our needs will seek expression and satisfaction, even ones that are seemingly inconsistent with our conscious understanding of who we would like to be. To be sustainable our personal integrity must include a realistic and holistic understanding of all parts of our personality. We must be aware of and integrate our shadow. When accepted and assimilated, our shadow can become a great source of growth, creativity, and balance. Thus, the focus of this chapter is on the theoretical and practical significance our shadow has in our life.

The Shadow

How do you typically describe who you are to yourself and others? Do you sometimes have thoughts or engage in behaviors that don't seem consistent with your typical ways of operating or understanding yourself? Do you wish you could change aspects of yourself? Are there parts of yourself that scare, annoy, or embarrass you? What behaviors or thoughts do you not allow yourself to entertain? Do you sometimes have dreams with characters that are engaged in behaviors you find repugnant and scary?

We all have standard ways of defining who we are, to ourselves and others. We have a *personal story* that defines our perceptions of our history, current life, and future plans. We have *identity markers* (e.g., age, gender, race, ethnicity, marital status, family, friends, job title, significant life events, etc.) that we use to ground and define our sense of self in the world. Each day when we wake up, and periodically throughout the day, we remind ourselves of our personal story and various identity markers. In this way our conscious sense of self is re-instated and re-affirmed on an ongoing basis. This conscious view of ourselves comprises what Jung referred to as our ego, the center of our consciousness. Our ego is the totality of our conscious self; it is our mental story of who we are.

While the ego is our conscious sense of self, which is typically infused with ideas of who we think we should be, the shadow comprises all we would like *not to be*. The shadow includes all things we have difficulty accepting about ourselves and what we find repulsive in others. We repress what we have learned to find unacceptable about ourselves into the shadow of our awareness. We often then project our shadow characteristics, qualities and attributes onto others. In other words, we deny ownership of certain needs, thoughts, behaviors or traits then disdainfully judge others who exhibit or represent those qualities. In fact, it is by exploring what annoys and scares us about others that we are often first able to discover the existence of our shadow.

For instance, if you define yourself as a highly responsible and hard-working person, behavior that you deem irresponsible would become part of your shadow—you might not allow yourself to be playful or spontaneous and would likely react strongly to others you view as lazy, unmotivated, or carefree. Conversely, if you highly value your spontaneous and laid-back persona, you may shy away from living on a schedule and may judge more structured people as "anal retentive types." If you see yourself as someone who takes a logical approach to life, emotional aspects of living will likely be banished into your shadow. If you prefer to avoid conflict, anger and assertive behaviors will become part of your shadow, and so on.

Interestingly, the shadow of people who see themselves in primarily self-deprecating ways contains positive thoughts about themselves. If an individual views herself as unworthy and inadequate, for example, more positive aspects of her self-concept would be banished into her shadow. Again, the shadow contains what our conscious view of ourselves will not allow or support.

Our shadow often presents itself to us in the form of people in our dreams. A number of years ago I had a recurring dream that provides a humorous example of how we can become aware of our shadow. I call the dream, *Dennis Rodman Won't Leave*, and have recounted it many times in seminars and lectures.

The dream always starts with a knock at the front door of my home during the evening. My wife, young child (my second wasn't born yet) and I are going though our typical evening routine: giving my daughter a bath and getting her ready for bed. I answer the door and Dennis Rodman is standing there (Dennis was a famous basketball player and show-business personality known for wild and outrageous behavior, on and off the court). In my dream he is dressed outlandishly and is severely intoxicated due to drugs and alcohol. He pushes his way into my house and starts to act bizarrely. He yells, flails around, and crashes into furniture and walls. My wife and child are upstairs and don't know that someone has entered our home. I try frantically to calm him down and get him out of my house before he can scare or hurt my family. I keep telling him that he has to leave, to no avail. His behavior continues to escalate, getting louder and more out-of-control, before he passes out on the floor just as I wake up—usually in a cold sweat!

My life-context during the time of this recurring dream is very telling. I was an assistant professor at Montana State University and focused on becoming tenured. I was working long hours at the University and at my private practice. We recently had our first child and purchased our first home; consequently I was feeling pressure to financially support my family and to succeed professionally. Our child was colicky and we weren't getting much sleep. When I wasn't working, I was home providing child care and trying to support my exhausted and stressed wife. Even when I was working I was feeling guilty because I knew that my wife was likely dealing with a crying, colicky baby. I had very little free time, physically or psychologically. Clearly I wasn't having much fun in my life. I often found myself resentful of friends and colleagues who didn't have children and had time to pursue self-oriented needs and interests. Although I feigned interest in and support of their adventures and exploits, I certainly didn't want to hear anything about anyone's wonderful Yoga class or spiritually-oriented trip to Peru!

Thankfully, I spoke with a colleague who helped me interpret my dream. What seems obvious to me now, but wasn't then, is that Dennis Rodman represented my shadow. He represented all that I was unable or unwilling to acknowledge in my life and myself: fun, spontaneity, carefree attitude, hedonism, and self-oriented gluttony. My consciousness was wrapped up in responsibility, control, achievement, and selfless giving. There was little room in my life for behaviors and experiences that didn't support my conscious, linear goals. As we will discuss throughout this chapter, this type of restricted sense of self is not sustainable. It will likely lead to judgment and resentment of self and others as well as acting in ways which contradict our core values.

How Shadows Form

The process of developing a shadow part of our personality is inevitable. It is virtually impossible not to do so. Thankfully, our shadow is not always extreme and problematic. As a matter of fact, when we become aware of and integrate our shadow, we feel a sense of sustainable wholeness and peace. However, our shadow will become problematic in our lives when our conscious sense of self becomes restricted beyond what is sustainable. As a general rule, the more restricted our sense of self becomes, the larger our shadow grows. Our personal integrity must be large enough to include all of who we are, or our shadow will expand and seek expression, oftentimes out of our conscious awareness.

Dichotomization of Experience

How do you define healthy versus unhealthy behaviors and experiences in your life? What language do you use to describe positive and negative experiences? Do you categorize experiences into good or bad?

We have a built-in tendency to categorize our experiences, to define them in ways that help us make sense of our world. Although plenty of gradation in our categorization occurs, our tendency is to dichotomize experiences into what is good or bad. For the most part, this is an adaptive tendency. If we couldn't discriminate among various experiences, between what may be harmful or beneficial for example, we would have great difficulty in our lives. Life would be much less safe and more unpredictable.

As is, we live in a somewhat unpredictable and constantly changing world. Events happen periodically, if not regularly, that challenge our sense of safety and stability: a diagnosis of a serious illness, a job lay-off, an automobile accident, a divorce, a destructive weather storm, a death, to name just a few. Even typical developmental changes, such as a child going off to school or an adult child getting married, raise our awareness of the change-ability of life.

When difficult and frightening events occur, we feel an increased sense of urgency to categorize our experiences. We want to understand why events happened so we can gain some control of our circumstances and avoid being afraid and unpleasantly surprised in the future. We want to control and predict our world. This tendency to dichotomize experiences into good and bad supports the development of the shadow, and as I discuss in the next section, plays a part in the development of our self-concept. Through the socialization process, we learn to incorporate good experiences and behaviors into our conscious sense of who we want to be while bad ones are repressed into the shadow.

Idealized Self

What are the characteristics of yourself or others that you most highly value? Do you judge yourself for not possessing more positive qualities? Which traits do you wish you had more of in yourself? Where did you develop your ideas about the traits and behaviors that you most admire?

To some extent, all of us have been given messages from our parents and society about how to live life. Just as it is adaptive for us to categorize our experiences, it is adaptive for us to learn from our parents about the world and to maintain connection with them. We are not a species that can survive on our own. As young children, we need the protection, guidance, and support of our caregivers. Thus our need for connection with and approval from others, especially parents, is hard-wired into our brains. In general, we want to please our parents and avoid disapproval.

Throughout our lives and especially during childhood and adolescence, we receive messages from our parents and society about the world and what types of behaviors are acceptable and valued and what types are not. We learn that some of our behaviors are deemed bad while others are good. We come to learn that some of our behaviors bring approval from parents while others bring criticism and punishment. Thus, our need for connection and approval tends to lead to an insidious compromise: we give up the vision and knowledge of our Real Self for the conditional love and approval of others.

In this context we engage in the process of forming our identity, our self-concept. We begin to define *who we are* and *who we are not*. We learn that we must banish some of our needs and the parts of ourselves that could endanger us or incur the wrath or disapproval of significant others, while we consciously embrace a sense of self which is based on these standards.

The dichotomy of acceptable and unacceptable behaviors thus becomes internalized and the *idealized self* is born and begins to grow. The idealized self is who we think we *should be*. It is who we think we need to be to gain the approval and acceptance of significant others. Even when the values and morals that are being internalized are positive and helpful, the process creates a restricted, conscious sense of self. To some extent, it is an inevitable aspect of the socialization process. Less acceptable aspects of ourselves become repressed from our consciousness. Our conscious sense of self then becomes synonymous with our internalized ideals, rather than our Real Self. The more that our conscious self becomes fused with our idealized self, the more of who we are gets shoved out of awareness and into the shadow of our personality. The narrower and more idealistic our conscious self becomes, the bigger our shadow becomes. And, the more we become alienated from the inner-generated, sustainable energy of our Real Self.

Sometimes, what becomes internalized is a reactive identity. That is, our conscious sense of self is formed in reaction to the internalization of standards and values that typically comprise the idealized self. In this situation, we adopt a persona of being bad. Pro-social values and morals are banished into our shadow, and our conscious sense of self is still restricted. Either way, the more restrictive our conscious sense of self is, the larger our shadow grows, thus leading to disconnection from our Real Self.

Restrictive Moral Visions

How rigid are the rules you use to govern your behavior? On what do you base your definition and standards for what is permissible? How do you determine if your personal mandates are your own or are externally imposed? How much of your personal integrity is infused with a rigid book of rules? How do you deal with your specific thoughts and needs that seem to be inconsistent with your personal integrity? Do you attempt to negate your needs rather than face and address all of who you are? To what degree do you judge your personal life-story through the lens of a restrictive moral vision?

Our humanity is the most unpredictable and frightening aspect of our own existence. Collectively and individually human beings are capable of a startlingly wide array of behaviors, from the wonderfully beautiful and creative to the horribly destructive and atrocious. For example, we can regularly become touched by genuine acts of love and kindness as well as aghast by the horrific behavior of individuals and groups of people that we hear about on news reports.

Although the behaviors of others scare us, the truly *most unsettling awareness is that each of us capable of all aspects of human behavior.* We would like to believe that we are not capable of certain thoughts and actions. We want to believe that we would act differently if we were in the same situation as others—we just couldn't possibly be capable of such things. We thus feel safe in our denial and righteousness, while pointing a judging finger at the behavior of others.

Our awareness (albeit limited) of our collective human potential for *good and evil* as well as the unpredictability of our world create a great deal of anxiety and a corresponding need to feel safe. As we have discussed, social and moral codes of conduct tend to serve the purpose of regulating and socializing behavior based on the dichotomized view of good and bad. Behaviors that are deemed socially acceptable are reinforced and held as the ideal while unacceptable and unpredictable behaviors are vilified.

So, as a society we deal with unpredictable and unsettling behaviors by creating rules of conduct, which can become restrictive moral imperatives. Individually, we also banish and negate some of our needs, especially the ones that will lead to disapproval from parents or remind us of our own potentials to engage in socially undesirable behaviors.

However, restrictive moral visions and the corresponding attempts to negate needs do not work well in the long-run. These strategies are simply not sustainable. All needs have a way of seeking expression, even if not directly. We can banish our needs for only so long before symptoms occur. Denial of our needs will typically lead to judgment of self and others, frustration, and eventually depression or acting out.

There are many examples of this process that can be seen in the media on a regular basis. Although shocked, we are less and less surprised when we hear about individuals in positions which exemplify moral righteousness who act out in ways that contradict their stated morals and bring great harm to themselves and others. This occurs across faiths and cultures: prominent figures who advocate morally righteous positions (e.g., politicians, civic leaders, law enforcement authorities, and church or spiritual leaders) caught engaging in socially unacceptable behaviors, oftentimes the very behaviors that they proclaim as immoral or illegal.

Consider the following clinical examples, which represent several common outcomes of having our personal integrity too closely aligned with our idealized self and a restrictive moral vision.

John grew up in a church and family that preached a restrictive moral vision based on a dichotomized view of good and bad. Throughout childhood, his consciousness was largely filled with feelings of lack and inadequacy based on the moral standards he was being taught. In adulthood, he continued to be an approval-seeker, especially with women and his relationship with God, never feeling as if he reached the standard of acceptability. His prayer life, for example, was filled with apologies and asking God for the strength to change and address his inadequacies. He settled for a love-restricted marriage, often blaming himself for his wife's lack of interest in him. He did his best to negate or restrict many of his needs. His shadow and his Real Self were almost totally out of his awareness. In addition to constant feelings of dissatisfaction with his life and marriage, he was chronically depressed and suffered with diffuse, chronic pain. Through psychotherapy he was able to stop internalizing shame and start getting angry (a forbidden, shadow emotion) about what was happening in his life. The anger became a motivating energy, which allowed him to take charge of his life and his own happiness.

Sarah also grew up in a church that preached a restrictive moral vision. Unlike John, she received a great deal of praise and often felt worthy of God's love. She knew very well the rules of the church and the expectations of her parents, and was capable of meeting the standards. She excelled in all areas of her life: school, church, friends, and family responsibilities. She was a shining star of virtues. Her conscious sense of self was synonymous with her idealized self: she was who she *should be*. During her college years, however, she started to have experiences and thoughts that challenged the dichotomized views of her upbringing. She began to realize that she was expert at pleasing others, but ignorant of her own values and needs. She became increasingly reactive to her parents' expectations and eventually left the church. She began to abuse drugs and alcohol and engage in sexually promiscuous behaviors. The more she acted out, the more her parents withdrew their love and attention. She also felt guilty about some of her behaviors. Sarah wasn't clear on the standards for her behavior or the origins of her guilt: Was the guilt in reaction to her parents' values or her own? She entered psychotherapy after a drug overdose almost killed her. She was confused, reactive, and angry. Thankfully, she was also ready to take ownership for her life. Like John, she was ready to *reclaim her Real Self.*

Marrying your Shadow

Do you feel as if your significant partner understands who you are? Do you feel *seen* by your partner? Can you be yourself with your partner? Do you have to hide parts of yourself in your relationship? Does your partner annoy, scare or frustrate you in repetitive ways? Does your partner possess characteristics that complement or balance your characteristics or tendencies? Do the characteristics or behaviors of your partner which first attracted you to him/her now irritate you? How often do you find yourself wishing that your partner would change certain characteristics or behaviors?

The quickest and most reliable way to learn about your shadow is by looking at your relationship history, and especially your spouse(s) or intimate partner(s). As I have said, to some extent, we all develop a view of who we are, who we want to be, and who we want not to be. Characteristics and experiences that are deemed unacceptable are repressed into the shadow, but they don't stop seeking expression. One way that our shadow is expressed is through our relationships. We unconsciously act out our un-integrated parts and experiences in our choice of intimate partners and the dance that develops over time.

We typically try to find intimate partners who are like us in some ways, but not like us in other ways. We want to be able to relate to the other person, but also want the person to expand us, to be different than we are. We are attracted to others who possess characteristics we find admirable or even scary because we have trouble embracing those characteristics. The unconscious hope is that we will be able to resolve our conflicts and integrate our shadow by being with someone who represents our un-integrated qualities and engages in some of our forbidden behaviors. Thus, the simplified answer to the question—What do I do with my unruly and unsightly shadow?—We repress it, and then marry it!

This process can work well in some instances, but is disastrous in others. The difference between growthful and perpetually painful relationships and outcomes can be captured by two words: *acceptance* and *change*. Couples who experience their relationship as a place to grow and integrate their shadows tend to accept each other while other couples suffer greatly by their attempts to change each other. I'll start with situations when it works well, before discussing examples of how and why it goes poorly.

Generally speaking, when intimate relationships go well, a secure attachment exists between the partners. The attachment is characterized by trust, care, respect, an ability to work through conflict, and mutual acceptance. To a large part, each partner feels known and accepted by the other. The relationship provides a secure base, from which each partner ventures out into the world, takes risks, and grows.

Like struggling couples, these individuals are drawn to each other, at least partially, because of each other's shadows. What is unfinished and underdeveloped in one, the other possesses to a greater extent. However, rather than trying to change the other as struggling couples often do, they maintain feelings of admiration and respect related to their differences. They can be role models for each other based on their mutual strengths. They each can learn new and more expansive and flexible ways of operating in and experiencing the world. Similarly, the secure base of the relationship provides a springboard to try out new behaviors and express various parts of themselves. For example, they can try out new careers or hobbies, possibly engage in creative outlets and relationships, or may intentionally expand their philosophical and spiritual beliefs and practices. This works best when they can trust that each will bring the energy of these experiences back into the relationship, for the benefit of both. Rather than being threatened by the other's growth and expansion, these partners are supportive and encouraging.

Obviously, this is easier said than done! Many couples struggle with these dynamics over the lifespan of their relationship. The struggles tend to focus on the fervent need to change their partner, which is really about an unconscious need to change parts of their own personality, the parts that have been deemed unacceptable. Thus, rather than being supportive of the other, they are threatened by certain behaviors or traits, most often the ones that represent their own shadow. Each partner becomes identified with a restrictive role (e.g., the pure one, the emotional one, the unpredictable one, the angry one, the responsible one, etc.) within the relationship, and maybe also their life in general. As their conscious sense of self becomes restricted, they move away from the unifying and integrating energy of their Real Self. Projection and projective identification start to take over in their relationship. Specifically, each partner projects his/her repressed shadow onto the other. The other partner identifies with the projection and then acts out from this restricted position.

The following are two clinical examples of this painful process; both represent couples who have lost touch with their Real Self, engaged in projective identification, and adopted restrictive, complementary roles based on their shadows. Each example revolves around the need for one or both partners to change, based on core relational themes, which occur commonly in individuals and couples who struggle with incorporating their shadows. Typical relational themes are highlighted, including control, trust, achievement, responsibility, purity, judgment, and emotional expression.

James and Judy. James first entered psychotherapy, saying that his wife told him he must attend counseling and change, or she was leaving. He wasn't clear about what needed to be changed, other than she "wants me to be more motivated." James had a moderately-high paying job. He was comfortable and didn't want to expend much energy trying to become promoted or trying to find a higher paying new job. He preferred to spend his weekends relaxing or engaging in fun activities, rather than working on the house or other projects. He wished Judy could "learn to relax" and stop trying to control him.

Judy was displeased about James' "complacency" in his career and in his life. She worked long hours and wanted to quit her job and have a baby. She was fearful that she couldn't count on James to "step up" and support them emotionally and financially when she stopped working outside the home. His laze-fare attitude activated her deep-seated feelings of insecurity, anxiety, and judgment.

James grew up in a family where he felt ignored by both parents: his father traveled extensively and his mother worked long hours in a professional job. A core message that he internalized from his childhood (in reaction to his parents' overworking) was: "there are more important things in life than work." He didn't want to become like his parents, yet they were his primary role models. Thus, he worked hard enough to succeed moderately, but also vilified working "too hard." To some extent, his achievement needs were repressed into his shadow. He preferred to see himself as "mellow and easy-going." He was largely satisfied with Judy making most of the decisions in their life.

Judy grew up in a single-parent family. Her father left when she was young and her mother struggled to raise children and support the family financially. A core message that she internalized from childhood was: "If you want something done, you can count on only yourself." Trusting others, especially men, was difficult for her. She was a driven person, who had succeeded at everything throughout her life. Her primary strategies were to work hard and stay in-control. She was regularly setting and achieving goals in her work and life. After working long hours during the week, her weekends were filled with chores, household projects, and preparation for the upcoming work week. She often found herself feeling judgmental of James's mellow attitude. Now that she wanted to have a baby, she felt vulnerable and panicked about whether she could trust him to support her. Her needs for fun, spontaneity, and relaxation were banished into her shadow.

James and Judy were acting from restricted positions. He projected his shadow needs for achievement and control onto Judy, while she projected her shadow needs for fun and spontaneity onto James. They had the potential to support each other in finding healthy balance and perspective and to integrate their shadows. Instead, resentment and frustration festered and grew. Still, Judy was unconsciously attempting to incorporate her shadow by wanting to have a child and quit her job (a very risky venture for her psychologically). Through her actions she was inviting James to help her integrate her shadow; however, she continued to utilize her familiar strategy of control as a way to manage her anxiety. The unresolved relational issues from each of their families of origin (e.g., neglect, loss, and abandonment) were directly contributing to the maintenance of their shadows and their restricted positions in their marriage.

Katy and Don. Katy and Don entered marriage therapy in crisis. Their ten-year marriage was hanging on by a thread. Both were saying they weren't sure whether they wanted to stay married. She had recently revealed that she had been having an affair for the past six months, and wasn't at all clear if she wanted to end it. She felt as if she "couldn't be herself" in the marriage. She stated that she was able to be much more "free and comfortable" when she wasn't with Don. In her view, he was emotionally distant and psychologically stifling. He was always "so good, did the right things, and had the right answers." She felt as if she couldn't measure up to his high standards, no matter how hard she tried. Now, she broke a shared rule (fidelity) and "would never be forgiven." Although she thought her relationship with Don may be over, she felt relieved the affair was out in the open, as were her feelings of dissatisfaction with her marriage. The one thing she was clear about was that she did not want to go back to business as usual; she couldn't go back to her life as it had been—no matter how much it hurt Don.

Don was shocked, hurt, and angry about the affair. He knew there had been distance in their relationship and was often irritated by Katy's "bouts of irrational emotion." He was also worried that she drank too much, at times. But, he never expected her to break his trust in such a hurtful way. His usual intellectual style was breaking down; he was experiencing more emotions and pain than he could remember ever feeling. He had worked hard and followed the "rules;" how could this happen? He wanted to file for divorce, but also believed that they had to make sound decisions for the kids, ages eight and five.

Katy grew up in a large, "close-knit" family. Her father was a functional alcoholic. He drank alcohol every evening, but never missed work. When he drank, he would disengage from the family and become unapproachable. Periodically, her father and mother would get into heated verbal debates about his drinking. She remembers feeling powerless and afraid for her mother's safety during these arguments. Her primary role in her family was to make everyone laugh; she distracted them from the obvious tension and struggle. Her emotions were always on her sleeve. She was drawn to Don because of his "stability," which gave her a sense of comfort and security. However, over time she felt increasingly "trapped" by Don's stoicism and psychological distance. Her usual gregarious nature was more and more subdued in their relationship.

Don grew up in a family with three children; he was the oldest. His mother was an active alcoholic until she began attending AA meetings when Don was a teenager. He described his mother as chaotic, disorganized, and prone to crisis, especially during the years before she stopped drinking. His father was largely unavailable, except when Don participated in sporting events or succeeded in activities and academics. Don's father never missed one of his games. Consequently, Don excelled at athletics and everything else he tried, in an attempt to gain his father's attention and approval. He felt responsible for bringing positive attention to his family. He also looked after his younger siblings when his mother was impaired by alcohol and his father was unavailable. He learned to master his emotions and approach life from a rational perspective. He was initially attracted to Katy because of her ability to make him laugh and help him "lighten up." However, over the course of their marriage he had become increasingly displeased about her "emotional instability and irresponsibility."

Like James and Judy, Katy and Don had adopted restricted positions. Both had developed compensatory strategies from their families of origin. Her role as the family comedian, and his as the responsible one, had evolved into restricted roles in their marriage. He became "the Saint" while she became "the adolescent." She projected her shadow needs for safety and predictability onto Don, while he projected his shadow needs for emotionality and rebelliousness onto Katy. Katy had unconsciously attempted to integrate her shadow and *help them both* by having an affair. Initially she felt more alive and was consequently unwilling to let go of the affair. However, her behavior was outside her own personal integrity and was not sustainable. But, the pain of the affair gave them the motivation to learn and grow. The affair was an opportunity to understand the depth of their shadows and how they became lost from their Real Self. Thus, they had an opportunity to resolve core relational dynamics from their childhoods, take ownership for their lives, and reclaim their Real Self.

Rick Johnson Ph.D.

Integration
The process of integrating our shadow is life-long. We can't do it just once and then be done. Our shadow will always exist as a repository of what is deemed unacceptable or is unfinished or underdeveloped in our personality and our life. However, we can become more centered and whole by understanding and embracing our shadow. Like the differentiation process, this involves the two continually repeating steps of awareness and ownership.

Awareness
The content of our consciousness is constantly changing; it ebbs and flows based on internal and external factors. We are constantly bombarded by demands of our life-contexts as well as our internal thoughts and needs. As I have discussed, we categorize and judge our experiences and needs, with some being deemed less acceptable or worthy than others. As our conscious sense of self and our corresponding behavioral options become restricted, our shadow grows. To counteract this restrictive process, we must become aware of the existence of our shadow. We must become aware of all of who we are and all of our various needs. Thus, the first step in the process of integrating your shadow is increasing your self-awareness.

A good place to start is by looking at your relationships. Take a moment to consider the various people in your life: intimate partners, family, friends, coworkers, etc. Who evokes strong emotions in you? Who rubs you the wrong way? Who scares you? Do you feel as if you are in a restricted role in any of these relationships? Of these people, picture a person in your mind that activates feelings within you. What feelings are arising in you? What does this person represent to you? What does this person do that you don't allow for yourself? It is likely that you are projecting some of your shadow onto this person—or any person with whom you have intense, judgmental feelings. It may also be that you are the recipient of his/her projections.

At this point, the goal is simply to increase awareness of when you become emotionally activated. Notice your discordant feelings about this person. Notice your desire for him/her to change in certain ways. When activated, simply pause and experience the feelings rather than banishing or acting on them. Listen to what your fearful, angry, or judgmental voice is saying. What might this voice be saying about you?

You can learn the most by considering how this person is acting out an underdeveloped or unfinished part of yourself. Try to become aware of what rules or restrictions may be defining what is allowable for you as it relates to this person. It may be that you are negating or restricting certain needs, which this person acts out more freely. Any person who evokes a strong response in you provides you with an opportunity to learn about your under-expressed needs.

As I have said before, *don't pathologize your needs—needs just are.* The important thing is that you become aware of your needs and how you are trying to get your needs met. Again, if you are unaware of your needs or vilify them, they will still attempt to seek expression and attainment. Being unaware of your needs is a recipe for acting out your shadow in ways you will likely regret. Awareness, on the other hand, leads to choice. You can therefore be much more intentional about how and when to meet your needs.

Ownership

Once your awareness begins to increase, the next step is ownership—taking responsibility for yourself and your needs.

Again, a handy way to increase ownership is to look at other people for whom you have judgmental feelings. As you become aware of who activates you, you should then turn your attention back to yourself, to your needs and your life. What can you learn about yourself from this other person? What do you think would happen if you would incorporate the very characteristics that generate your judgmental feelings? How would your life be different if you didn't pathologize those needs? What would happen if you took ownership for all of who you are? Do any fears emerge as you ponder this?

Rather than being victimized or offended by the disowned characteristics, try to incorporate them as your own. Imagine utilizing the energy of those "unacceptable" characteristics for your own life. Visualize the denied characteristics. Now own them in a way that stays true to your integrity. For example, if you are offended by another person's "laziness and immaturity," you are most likely not meeting your needs for relaxation, fun and spontaneity. Don't be afraid of the *laziness monster;* it will teach you about your unmet needs as well as your tendency to overwork. You don't have to meet your relaxation and enjoyment needs the same way the other person does; you can choose how you will meet your needs. Just make sure that your integrity is not being hampered by a restrictive moral vision.

Another example would be if it is difficult for you to tolerate someone who acts in a brash or demanding manner with others. First you might notice your discomfort with this person, and consider how you have dealt with this discomfort. Have you avoided this person, or even tried to change him/her in the past? If instead, you are able to embrace the energy of this person, you will learn how you can become more whole and integrated. Maybe you don't need to be brasher, but you can probably use the strength and assertiveness of this energy.

At some point, if you practice this type of awareness and ownership, you will even become thankful for those that annoy, frustrate, or scare you. They will become your teachers. They will teach you about what you are avoiding and need to incorporate into our own life. You will be thankful for the awareness that these teachers live within you, in your shadow. You will learn that you can be assertive or spontaneous or any other denied characteristic and you can do it in a way that is congruent with your personal integrity. You can meet your needs and be true to your convictions.

Many people, when they allow themselves to imagine a life driven by their needs in this way, have fears about losing control and engaging in immoral or self-centered behaviors. Typically, their fears focus on becoming lazy or hedonistic. For example, they picture that they might lie around the house all day, eating chocolates. Maybe they would allow themselves to become addicted to sex or drugs, etc. In actuality, these fears tend to be unfounded, and contribute to the development of un-integrated shadows. In other words, because of these fears, individuals tend to banish these needs and work hard to avoid activating their unwanted potentials. In contrast to their fears, most people make balanced life-choices, especially when they are based on self-awareness and the wisdom of their Real Self.

To illustrate this integration process, consider the following clinical example. Dave, a 35 year-old man, grew up as an only child in a middle-class, Christian family. His parents were intellectuals who expressed a strong faith and stressed nonviolence and caring for others. A strong interpersonal theme in his family was avoidance of conflict. Disagreements were rare. Being gracious and accommodating to others were prized values in his family.

As an adult, Dave viewed himself as a caring, "good guy." He never wanted to be the center of attention or seen as too needy. He married a woman who grew up in a chaotic, alcoholic family. She was regularly upset emotionally and was drawn to Dave's stability. He was drawn to her ability to be open with her emotions, since he felt detached from his own. Over time, Dave and his wife focused on raising their four children; their marriage became stale and lifeless, although neither would acknowledge it initially.

Dave entered therapy due to series of events. He had started to experience debilitating depression, which was impacting his work performance. He had just received a poor evaluation at work. He also admitted that he had been frequenting strip clubs, although he indicated that didn't know why he was going. In therapy, Dave was able to recognize how many of his needs were being negated and repressed into his shadow. All of his expansive characteristics and needs, including assertiveness and sexuality, were being denied and vilified. His restrictive moral vision of conflict avoidance and accommodation were squeezing the life out of him and his marriage. He was being a "good guy," but was acting out his shadow in ways that were contradicting his integrity. His depression was a sign that he was not living his life based on his Real Self. Rather, he was desperately trying to live up to his idealized vision.

Thankfully, his self-awareness began to increase. He reported dreams in which characters were engaged in bold and repugnant behavior that he would never consciously allow for himself. These characters represented his shadow. He began to see how he was living as a restricted-self, not a whole-self. He began to recognize his tendency to avoid conflict and accommodate others, to the exclusion of his own needs and wants, which led to his shadow acting out in ways far beyond his personal integrity. He stopped going to strip clubs, but was able to express those forbidden needs in ways that were more in-line with his personal integrity, such as exercise, work achievement, and increased sexuality with his wife. He began to listen to the voice and feel the presence of his Real Self.

In addition to individual psychotherapy, Dave and his wife went into marital counseling where they were able to grow and learn through the crisis as a couple. Although she was hurt and scared by his deceit and actions related to the strip clubs (which reminded her of her father), she also felt relieved and empowered by the honesty. Over time, they both began to reclaim the disowned and denied parts of their personalities. Consequently, they each felt more alive and engaged in their marriage and their lives.

This example illustrates the power of awareness and ownership of all of who we are. An awareness of who we think we must be (the idealized self) and who we don't want to be (the shadow) allow the Real Self to emerge into consciousness. Our shadow will continue to seek expression, a process that represents our Real Self's unconscious attempt to become whole, especially in the face of narrow and restrictive visions. Although it may show itself in ways that are unsustainable and outside of our integrity, our *health is trying to emerge*. When our consciousness fills with the presence of our Real Self, we make choices that are congruent with our integrity and incorporate all aspects of who we are. We thus claim our lives and feel a sense of balance and congruency.

As we have previously discussed, your focus should be on living a *value-driven life*, one that takes into account all of your needs. A value-driven life is based on awareness and choice. Behaviors are chosen based on internal values and needs rather than externally imposed rules. If they look deeply, most people find that their values include responsibility, caring for others, and accomplishing goals, as well as fun, freedom, and pleasure. Finding a healthy balance of your various needs takes much intentionality; when you are able to do so your life feels like your own. Your life is based on a sustainable sense of personal integrity. Your fear will naturally decline. Your personal power and integrity will naturally increase. This is about living your life in accordance with the wisdom and integrating energy of your Real Self. So, rather than living a *self-centered life*, live a *Real Self-centered life!*

Chapter 9
Self and No-Self

"Carrying body and soul and embracing the one, Can you avoid separation?"

Lao Tsu, *Tao Te Ching*

Throughout this book, I have referred to the idea of a core self, the Real Self. I have also discussed parts of our personality: the idealized self, the shadow, the ego, etc. These conceptions of self have been developed largely within a Western psychological frame of reference. In fact, much of Western psychotherapy practice tends to focus on identifying and building a person's conception of self. For example, psychotherapists and counselors regularly focus on exploring and improving their clients' self-concept and self-esteem. The central aspect of increasing differentiation, a likely therapy goal, is the development of a separate sense of self and associated psychological boundaries within relationships.

Other paradigms, including some spiritually-based points of view, challenge the notion of a separate self, and sometimes, the idea of the existence of a self at all. From these perspectives, the psychological focus on the development of the self is problematic. In short, self-focus either perpetuates a person's difficulties by supporting a false or distorted view of self and separateness, or becomes the problem because it supports self-centeredness.

The differences between Western psychological and spiritual/philosophical views of the self can generate difficulties when

Rick Johnson Ph.D.

trying to integrate these worldviews. In this chapter I consider various philosophical and practical views of the self. The dilemmas inherent in these views as well as an integrated model are presented. Rather than being antagonistic, psychological and spiritual views can support and complement each other. The Real Self, which is our spiritual center, is again the unifying concept.

No-Self

How do you view what defines and designates who you are? To what degree do you see yourself as separate from everything else? Is your sense of self derived from physical or psychological boundaries between you and others? How do you explain differences in the way you act in different situations and contexts? Could it be that you have various parts to your personality that emerge in different contexts? Do you believe you have a *false self* and a *core self*? What role does consciousness play in your definition of self?

Eastern Philosophical Perspectives

Eastern philosophical thought is vast and broad. Although significant differences exist among Eastern paradigms, and even within Buddhist traditions, there is a common theme related to ideas of *no-self*. In fact, the ideas of no-self are most associated with Eastern philosophies and religions. Whereas Western thinking tends to focus on each individual as a distinct self, Eastern philosophy, and Buddhism in particular, views the idea of a separate self as a false belief.

A central part of the wisdom of the Buddha's enlightenment focuses on the ideas of interconnection and *anatman,* the Sanskrit word meaning non-self. These concepts illustrate the idea that we don't have an independent existence that is separable from everything else. Everything in the world is interconnected. We are part of a vast web of particles and energy that intermingle with everyone and everything. Any action we make occurs within a larger context and affects all parts of that context, even if not obviously. In other words, when we act, it ripples out like a drop of water in a pond, although the effects may be subtle and difficult to perceive. And it isn't just our actions. Our thoughts, and our very being, occur within and affect this larger energy field.

In Buddhism, the idea that all things are interconnected is sometimes referred to as *dependent origination*. This principle has three major parts. First, all things come into existence as a result of conditions, not just in isolation. Second, a whole thing exists based on the interaction of its parts, again not in isolation. Third, all things remain in existence only as they interact with everything else that is or could be related to them. Thus, nothing exists as an independent entity.

Dependent origination implies that interconnectedness occurs not only spatially, but temporally. Events that have happened in the past set in motion certain conditions, options, and expectations. For example, our ancestors have deeply influenced our lives, even if we have never met them in person. Their choices and experiences, years before we were born, have influenced the circumstances of our lives in many ways, including genetically, financially, educationally, geographically, and relationally. Many, if not most, philosophers argue strongly that historical and current life circumstances and conditions are far more powerful in our lives than we tend to believe, quite possibly even more powerful than our own free will. The options that we have freedom to choose are really quite limited, due to the choices of many others and the conditions that these choices and circumstances have created. Even though our brains trick us into believing we have a tremendous amount of free will, our capacity to choose is extremely limited.

Another related aspect of non-self is the Buddhist concept of *sunyata*, emptiness of self. This tends to be understood as emptiness of a separate self. But, this concept also represents the idea that we are empty, that we truly have no self. Thus, not only are all things interconnected, but they possess no intrinsic identity.

From this perspective, all we are is our experience in the moment, our consciousness. What we perceive as our self is a false construction. It is our constructed self that we affirm by reminding ourselves of the various labels that we use to define a self. The most common forms of self-identification include possessions, job title, social and financial status, physical attributes and appearance, achievements and accomplishments, abilities, relationship status and history, and various belief systems. These self-identifications, or ego-identifications, as they are sometimes called, are not really who we are, but are labels and mental constructions.

Scientific discoveries at the atomic and subatomic levels have provided support and credibility to ideas of no-self by revealing that all things are mostly empty. What seems solid, including our bodies and hard objects, are actually almost completely empty space. Physicists have demonstrated that great distances occur between atoms in relation to their size and that atoms contain almost nothing, except empty space. What creates the sense of solidity and separation among things is more like an energy field than an actual solid substance.

Thus, from a Buddhist (and Quantum physics) perspective, the idea that we are separate and distinct is an illusion, and is also an incorrect and dangerous delusion. It fosters a mindset of objectification of people and things, which leads to unhealthy attachments to some things and disregard for others, rather than an understanding that we are part of all things. Unfortunately, this mindset also supports the assumption that we can act with limited consequence to our larger context.

A relevant example, which a friend pointed out to me, is how driving in a car can provide a basic lesson on interconnection. The actions and decisions of all drivers affect the safety and well-being of many people. If one person acts, intentionally or by accident, in a careless manner while driving a car, the consequences can be severe and far-reaching. A serious car accident can change not only the lives of the drivers and passengers, but of the bystanders, emergency responders, family members, friends, and even the people who read about the tragedy in the newspaper the next morning. The effects can ripple far beyond what we normally consider. We truly are part of an interconnected web that is well beyond our normal comprehension.

Existential Perspectives

As with Eastern philosophy, Existentialism represents the ideas of various thinkers rather than a unified paradigm. I will not attempt to summarize the variety of systems of thought associated with Existentialism. However, some unification around the idea of no-self can be formulated.

Unlike Buddhism which embraces interconnectedness, Existentialists tend to view us as separate, often alienated, and ultimately responsible for our own existence. However, similar to Buddhism, our sense of self (i.e., ego) is primarily seen as a false self. Our typical believe system about who we are is viewed as a compensatory creation. It exists in reaction to our largely unconscious sense that we inherently lack meaning and permanence.

Specifically, our chronic fear of death as well as our discomfort and struggle with meaninglessness create constant low-level anxiety and periodic panic. The anxiety associated with living life in the face of our precariousness and inevitable death motivates us to create a compensatory identity. Thus, Existential anxiety is the root of our self-deception. When we believe that we actually are the various labels that we use to define ourselves, we are in a state of denial and are distracting ourselves from the inevitability of death and our struggles with attaining authentic meaning in our lives.

From this perspective, the primary danger occurs from believing that our false, constructed self is a true self. Our view of self, with its various identity markers, needs to be deconstructed. That is, our self-identity needs to be examined, and self-deception needs to be removed. So, although Existentialism doesn't directly say that we are empty and have no self, like Buddhism does, it reminds us of a similar point: we are prone to self-deception and the tendency to create a false sense of self, which compensates for our chronic, low-level awareness of our impermanence and foundational meaninglessness and groundlessness.

Christian Perspectives

Although not widely known for espousing views of no-self, Christianity provides several ideas relevant to the discussion. Most notably is the focus on selflessness versus selfishness and God's plans versus individual plans. Again, whereas Western psychotherapy tends to address each individual's wants and needs, Christianity tends to see this self-focus as missing the bigger picture and potentially quite problematic.

A strong Christian belief is the notion that we are prone to selfish thoughts, desires, and behaviors. Too much self-focus can lead to selfishness and disregard for others. This message proposes that the path to growth and salvation includes giving up selfish tendencies and living a life based on a higher purpose.

This perspective has, at times, led to a disavowal of the physical body and self-oriented striving as well as a devaluing of material possessions. The body is seen as the repository of unhelpful urges and sensations, which need to be contained. Material possessions, which are based on self-needs, are seen as an unsustainable attempt to replace the sense of lack that is created in the absence of embracing God. Similar to the Existential view, our self-oriented thoughts and behaviors are understood to be compensatory. While Existentialism would propose that we are compensating for a lack of meaning and the fear of our inevitable death, Christianity attributes our lack of meaning and fear specifically to a disconnection from God's love.

From this perspective, we need to replace our individual wants and plans with God's plans for us. Our individual plans will be inherently selfish and lacking perspective. Thus, our plans are doomed to be a struggle and unsatisfying over time. Getting clear about God's plans for us provides the guiding focus and direction across all areas of our lives. Although I think some parts of this message can be problematic, especially when taken to extremes, the main idea is that our lives will work much better when our choices and actions are congruent with God's energy, Spiritual Energy. This specific message is compatible with central ideas already presented in this book and will be expanded upon later in this chapter.

Multicultural Perspectives

Multiculturalism, which includes views on gender and ethnic diversity, has recently been embraced as an essential paradigm

Rick Johnson Ph.D.

for psychology. Western psychotherapy historically has taken an excessively individualistic and male-centric approach to understanding and intervening in clients' lives. The need to conceptualize clients' issues from a more systemic and culturally-sensitive perspective is now viewed as a necessary part of providing effective mental health and counseling services. There are several components and movements within the multicultural field. I will focus narrowly on the aspects most related to no-self.

As I have stated, Western psychology has traditionally given greater importance to individual self-development than to interpersonal relatedness and context. The focus has tended to be on developing a separate self, punctuating the development of autonomy and independence as markers of health and maturity. A relational focus, which is more associated with females than males, has tended to be pathologized and viewed as less mature than characteristics such as separateness and autonomy.

Thankfully, gender-sensitive models for conceptualizing human development have challenged this pathologizing view of a relational orientation. For example, contemporary relational theories have proposed that the self develops in an interpersonal context. How we define ourselves is inextricably linked to what is mirrored to us through countless relational experiences, especially with parents and other family members. Our very idea of who we are and what we can expect from the world is formed in relationships. Our relationships become internalized as templates or blueprints of self, others, and self vis-à-vis others, which we carry with us throughout our lives. So, there is no self without others. The self doesn't develop or exist in isolation, ever.

In addition to gender-oriented models, ideas of individuality and togetherness must be considered from an ethnic diversity perspective. Concepts of the self have been challenged as less relevant in some non-Western cultures. The self holds different meanings, values, and visions across cultures. For example, some non-Western cultures have a much more group-oriented consciousness than is typically understood in Western societies. The emphasis in group-oriented cultures tends to be on cooperation and socially oriented values as opposed to competition and individualistic values. In group-oriented cultures the self doesn't exist conceptually as a separate entity. Consciousness of self is always in relation to family (including ancestors), community, geography, and culture.

An Integration of Self and No-Self

What is the nature of the self? How can we have a self and have no-self at the same time? Is our experience of self inherently compensatory, simply trying to fill a void or a sense of lack? Does connecting to our core self mean we are disconnecting from God, Spiritual Energy? Is self-focus synonymous with selfishness? Is a self conception incompatible with a social and relational consciousness?

Transcending Self

It will be helpful to begin the discussion by reviewing some of the concepts of self that I have mentioned thus far. Specifically, I look at the core of who we are, our very essence, as the Real Self. As the seat of our spiritual potential and a deep pool of inner wisdom, our Real Self contains not only our individual knowledge, but also taps into the ancestral wisdom of the collective unconscious, as described by Jung. Furthermore, the essence and life breath of our Real Self is God's life breath. It is the Holy Spirit, or Spiritual Energy, within us. And, Spiritual Energy is not just within us, it is within everything. It is what binds all of us and everything together.

Rick Johnson Ph.D.

Every other state of consciousness, outside the Real Self, is compensatory. Our consciousness can be distracted by and filled with many forms of mentalization and self-identifications. Our minds can be consumed by endless thoughts and mental noise. For example, we can believe that our ego-driven, personal story and self-identifications are real, that we truly are our occupations, socioeconomic status, material possessions, etc. We can also lose ourselves in the consciousness of our idealized self—who we think we should be, if we are to be acceptable and adequate to ourselves and/or others. Simply put, our consciousness can be so wrapped up in our ego and ego-ideal that we come to believe that this is who we are, which creates a false and deluded sense of self.

The Buddhist and Existential views of no-self can first and foremost be understood as *no ego or idealized self.* These compensatory states of consciousness need to be deconstructed; they are a false and fragile self. They keep us stuck in a consciousness of separateness and underlying fear. We need to empty ourselves of these self-identifications and experience the fullness and energy of our Real Self. It may sound like an oxymoron—emptying oneself as a way to experience fullness. However, by emptying ourselves of ego-based identifications and idealizations we open ourselves to the fullness of our Real Self and Spiritual Energy.

The Real Self is filled with Spiritual Energy. When we connect with this Energy, we become calm, centered, and clear. Spiritual Energy flows through us, as it does all things. It is the interconnecting force. It allows our consciousness to be able to see and experience the interconnection between all things. When we are awake to Spiritual Energy, we are filled with God's life breath—we are not alone.

Try not to get caught up in or reactive to the words: God,

Spiritual Energy, etc. They are just words used to convey an experience, a connection with the divine Source. When we let go of the words and enter the experience it creates space for Spiritual Energy to emerge into our consciousness. This state of being fosters a deep connection with everything around us.

When we make decisions and take action from this consciousness, we are inherently unselfish. We are *self-in-relation* to all else. The boundary between self and all else melts away. Thus, contrary to the fears of selfishness and being self-centered, when we connect with the Spiritual Energy that emanates from our Real Self, we are compassionate with others and considerate in our actions. Our plans and wishes are connected to the wisdom of Spiritual Energy. We do not forsake God's plans for our individual plans, as some Christians fear. That happens only when we are not connected to our Real Self and, therefore, our plans are ego-driven. *Turning inward to our Real Self and our Spiritual Energy is connecting with God.* We connect with our *soul's intentions,* which are God's intentions for us. Our lives become in-flow with the Spiritual Energy within and around us.

When we are removed from Spiritual Energy, it is like being naked in the world. We are fearful and alone. Our compensatory self and ego-identifications can quiet the fear, but for only so long. Most of us have a vague sense that there is more to life than what our ego tells us; there is more to who we are than we consciously know. Eventually, we awaken and begin to realize that our ego-driven views of self are false and fragile.

So, why do we give up the clarity and centeredness of Spiritual Energy for an unsustainable compensatory self? The primary reasons for losing touch with our Real Self, as were discussed in Chapter Five, are fear and reactivity. Life is full of fear, and the ego is a magnet for it. Fear drives the ego to create a false self.

Rick Johnson Ph.D.

The ego is bolstered by compensatory behaviors, like achieving social status and amassing possessions, which run rampant when we are insecure and anxious. Fear drives us to act reactively rather than thoughtfully. However, the fear-driven ego will soften and recede in the face of Spiritual Energy.

As we reclaim our Real Self and allow Spiritual Energy to emerge, fear and ego identifications dissipate. In its place we experience a sense of presence within us, and around us. We have a feeling of being home in our bodies and deeply connected to our own being. And at the same time, we experience a connection with everyone and everything around us. Thus, we can have a self and no-self at the same time. We have a sense of *self* (Real Self) and of *no-self* (interconnection), simultaneously. Ideas of separateness drop away. Our consciousness embraces Spiritual Energy as the presence within us and within all things as well as the interconnecting Energy between all things. Our breath is the breath and Energy within and among all things. Our breath is God's life breath. It is the Holy Spirit, our Buddha nature. It flows through and among all things.

Reclaiming your Real Self

The process of reclaiming your Real Self is often a developmental one, which evolves over time. In childhood, we begin the process of defining a self, looking to our parents and siblings primarily, to see and understand ourselves through their eyes. We learn about our wants as well as our likes and dislikes. We learn what is acceptable to others, what brings approval, and what brings scorn.

The process expands and intensifies during adolescence as we become deeply influenced by friends and societal views of what is cool or hip. Our realization of our idealized self increases;

we learn more about what is acceptable, even as we don't fit well into this mold. We struggle to be true to ourselves and be accepted by family, friends, and society. The shadow continues to grow as a way to deal with the mismatch between who we are and who we want to be; it grows as the repository of unacceptable parts of ourselves.

In the struggle to define a self in the face of familial and societal expectations and ideas of who we should be, the ego takes hold. We develop a personal story of who we are, complete with ever expanding ideas of what that means. We pick up self-labels, ego-identifications. These serve the purpose of creating a self, albeit somewhat false and misguided, which keeps us afloat in the world. We use our ego-driven view of self as a structure and scaffolding in the face of meaninglessness and groundlessness. Many people simply do not have the psychological and spiritual maturity to be aware of their ego-driven views of self, much less to deconstruct these views. The Buddhist-based adage, *you can't lose your self until you have a self,* is very relevant during this stage of development.

Most people begin adulthood with a strongly entrenched personal story and sense of *I, me,* and *mine.* Boundaries tend to be a primary issue for people at this stage. They tend to struggle to define themselves in relation to others, either over- or under-emphasizing separateness of self. Some of their identity includes the Real Self, but most of it is ego-driven and compensatory. The degree to which they have experienced life challenges, such as loss, trauma, and unhealthy role models, is often predictive of how disconnected they are from their Real Self. The more we utilize compensatory behaviors and ego-driven views of self, the more lost from our Real Self we tend to be.

Thus, we all venture forth into adulthood with our toolbox

of compensatory strategies and a corresponding cognitive map of who we are and what to expect from the world. The process of defining and implementing a self continues: educational and employment choices, relationships, and various life-experiences. Most of us are simply struggling to survive in our lives, financially and psychologically. To some extent, fear is the motivating force that drives us to continue the compensatory patterns in our life. For some, these patterns and strategies predominate for the rest of their lives.

Even while fear and an ego-driven view of self are largely in charge, *health is trying to emerge.* Health is the force and intentions of the Real Self. It is how we would live our lives if we were led by the Real Self and Spiritual Energy rather than driven by fear and compensation. It is the wisdom and Energy that is trying to help us resolve the blocks in our lives, which cloud our vision and keep the presence of our Real Self out of our awareness.

Somewhere in adulthood, most of us become increasingly aware that our ego-based view of self and our well-worn compensatory strategies are not sustainable or all of who we are. We may start to have more frequent glimpses of our Real Self or some other connection with Spiritual Energy that sparks an awakening within us. We also may have experiences which humble us and overwhelm our usual protective strategies and view of self. The usefulness of our personal, ego-based identity begins to run its course.

For many of us, this awakening happens around mid-life. There is a re-consideration of how we have defined ourselves and our lives. Adults in this stage can become reactive against the institutions of their lives, such as their relationships and career choices. Although this can be a tumultuous time, the underlying impetus is the Real Self emerging. Health is trying to emerge into consciousness.

This is a time to try out new behaviors and experiences and to be open to the possibilities of life. It is often described by individuals as an attempt to be more honest and real with themselves and others in their life. This can be quite threatening to the individual and his/her relationships, especially when it is coupled with a lack of awareness. If individuals are unconscious to the underlying intentions of their Real Self, as many people are, their behaviors will be more like reactive flailing rather than thoughtful action. In this case, marriages, friendships, and careers can sometimes become sacrificial lambs. In some situations this is necessary, while in many others it is unnecessary and very unfortunate.

Some individuals engage in this mid-life process in dramatic fashion while others are more subtle. Either way, it is important to realize what underlying intentions and questions are emerging. What core questions are being asked and acted out? What issues or dynamics are trying to be resolved? What is the definition of health that is emerging? What are the honesty and integrity that underlie the behaviors and needs?

Again, even your impulsive and seemingly unproductive behaviors are being motivated largely by a need to resolve past blockages and to reclaim your Real Self. The key to successfully utilizing the momentum and intentions of this process are to be in-touch with Spiritual Energy. Accessing the wisdom of your Real Self and Spiritual Energy provides the guiding vision you need to harness the underlying motivations. Difficult choices may have to be made as you re-consider the activities and relationships in your life. Sustainable decisions about what is life-affirming versus life-detracting can be made only by your Real Self. Otherwise, you will likely continue to make reactive and unenlightened choices.

As I have said, it is imperative to become aware of what is really emerging. Many times it is not the surface choice (e.g., whether to stay with a job or relationship) that truly matters, but a deeper need to resolve what is unfinished and unresolved in your life. Remember, *health is trying to emerge.* Utilize its energy and intentions to grow and more fully inhabit your life. Utilize your Real Self and Spiritual Energy to ground yourself in your body and to attain clarity and wisdom about what health is for you. The following example will help to illustrate this entire process.

Donna grew up in the Rocky Mountain west on a farm. Her parents were traditional in their gender-roles and Christian in their religious beliefs. She had an idyllic childhood in many ways. She was close to her family, including her older brother and younger sister. She remembers being happy and content in her home and school-life throughout her childhood. She has fond memories of playing in the barn with her siblings and riding the tractor with her father. The expectations of her were clear, and she was able to meet those expectations most of the time. Verbal expressions of love and appreciation were rare in her family, but she knew she was loved by both parents.

The first signs of difficulty began to emerge during adolescence when she would express points of view that were contrary to her parents' views. She was startled on several occasions with the intensity of her parents' reactions to her thoughts and questions. She quickly learned that differences in opinion, especially about religion, were perceived by her parents as threatening and rebellious. Thus, she became adept at suppressing her feelings and needs that she thought might offend or create discomfort for others. She became a master at conflict-avoidance while denying parts of herself. Her questions and concerns about her parents' religious views remained largely unaddressed and avoided.

By the time she went off to college (one hour drive from home), she had never had a serious intimate relationship or even dated. She was sheltered and largely living her life through the eyes of her idealized self. In her mind, being a "good Christian" meant waiting for the right man before dating or engaging in sexual intimacy. She got good grades, worked a part-time job, and went home almost every weekend. Her primary compensatory strategies continued to be conflict-avoidance and suppression of almost all of her self-oriented needs. Her shadow was far out of her awareness.

Shortly after receiving her undergraduate degree, she began a graduate program in the human services field. Her parents were openly critical of this; they didn't see the point of graduate school. They wanted her to get married and return to live near home. She began to feel a great amount of pressure to live up to the idealized vision of a traditional marriage and family life.

During this time she met, Derrick. He also grew up in a farming family. He was divorced, which was contrary to her family's values, but seemed to be "someone her parents would like." Derrick charmed her with promises of support and love. Shortly after meeting him, she invited him to meet her parents. He convinced her parents that he loved Donna and wanted to be her husband. The parents approved, and they were married within three months.

Soon after they were married, Donna found out she was pregnant. Unfortunately, almost as soon as the ring was on her finger, Derrick began to treat her with disrespect and disregard. He started drinking heavily, staying out all night, and acting in controlling and demeaning ways towards her. She went to her doctor's visits for her pregnancy without him. He frequently lost or quit his jobs, and was unemployed much of the time.

Donna hid the truth of her marriage and her feelings about it from her family and friends. She didn't want to disappoint or worry them. She became increasingly isolated in her pain and shame. She had stopped attending church, largely based on his criticism of her attendance, which led to further isolation. She continued with her usual compensatory behaviors of conflict-avoidance and suppression of her needs, even in the face of Derrick's hurtful behavior and her great pain. Derrick was the epitome of who she didn't want or allow herself to be. In very bold and painful ways he acted out her shadow.

In some ways she can thank Derrick. His behavior was so outrageous that she was eventually prompted to action, which ignited her differentiation and growth process. His mistreatment of her became a catalyst for health to emerge within her. If he had been just moderately disregardful, she likely would have put up with it indefinitely. However, his indifference and disregard was also extended towards their baby daughter, which triggered something for her. Although she wasn't feeling entitled to much kindness from him, when he rejected their daughter, she became more empowered.

It started slowly, but built in strength—her connection to her Real Self. Donna went from living in accordance with her parents' wishes, to living with Derrick's indifference. But, her strategies of conflict-avoidance and need-suppression were running their course. They simply couldn't quell the growing dissatisfaction within her. She couldn't stand it anymore. Encouraged by friends who began to question how Derrick treated her, she started to see a psychotherapist. In fits and starts she began to reclaim her Real Self.

The voice within her reminded her of her worth. Her Real

Self spoke with increasing clarity about her truth—what was life-affirming versus life-detracting in her life. She was finding her voice and starting to speak it out loud. First, she began setting boundaries with Derrick, and demanding that he treat her and their daughter with more respect. When he didn't, she found the courage to tell her family about her marriage and her unhappiness.

Initially her parents told her to try harder and lectured her about not giving-up. Her therapist helped her express herself clearly to her parents, and for the first time assertively disagree with their advice. Over time, they expressed their sorrow about her failing marriage and validated her experience. With her parents' blessing and her new found strength, she eventually left Derrick.

She finished graduate school and found employment that utilized her skills and passions. With some successes under her belt, she continued to find her voice with her parents. Their support was vital to her, but their judgment of her was at times oppressive. She needed to continue with her differentiation process and stake out her own life. Over time, she was able to maintain a strong connection with them while also being more able to differ with them and assert her independence when appropriate. Although her life was not perfect, for the first time she was living her own life rather than someone else's.

At this point, Donna had challenged her attachment to her idealized self and had moved down the path of differentiation and ownership for her life. She had defined a self in her relationships and had strong and more frequent experiences of her Real Self. Her awareness and utilization of her shadow had increased, mostly in the form of strong convictions, clearer boundaries, and assertiveness.

Interestingly, the religious and spiritual questions from her adolescence were resurfacing, but in a more mature way. At this time in her life, what did she believe about her faith? How could her spiritual beliefs and practices play a greater role in her life and growth?

She began to be open to various forms of spirituality, including her Christian roots. The experience was qualitatively different than when she was a child, however. Her faith matured and developed. She discovered a sense of presence in herself and her life. She had moved to a place where she was conscious of how her Real Self was aligned with Spiritual Energy. She began to live a value-driven life, where she was in charge. Her spiritual practice nourished and informed her life and her decisions.

As happens to many of us, the very painful struggles in Donna's life became the catalyst for her growth. Her marriage, as miserable as it was, prompted her to search for her Real Self. Health was always trying to emerge, but had been largely unconscious. Her Real Self was always there, waiting to be remembered and reclaimed.

Because of her unhappy marriage she learned to assert herself not only with Derrick, but also with her parents, friends, and co-workers. The core questions that she was unconsciously attempting to resolve rose to the forefront of her awareness. Questions such as: Who am I? Can I have needs? Am I entitled to a voice? If I assert myself will I be rejected? As health emerged, she resolved these core questions and reclaimed her Real Self.

Psychotherapy helped Donna a great deal on this journey, as it can for many people. Spiritually-sensitive psychotherapy, in particular, can assist people with this developmental process by helping them reclaim their Real Self, connect with Spiritual Energy, and utilize their struggles to embrace health as it emerges in their life. This process will be expanded upon in the next chapter.

Chapter 10

How Spiritually-Oriented Psychotherapy Helps

"It is the client's self-healing capacities and resources that are responsible for resolution of problems and for change in everyday life and in any form of psychotherapy."

Arthur Bohart and Karen Tallman,
How Clients Make Therapy Work

In what ways does psychotherapy help people feel better and function more effectively in their lives? How can it help people who are feeling *lost* reclaim their Real Self? Are some therapy approaches better than others? What are the factors that really account for client change in therapy? How can spiritually-oriented psychotherapy help? How can you get the most from your therapy experience?

There are an extraordinary number of different therapy models that are available, with each one claiming to have solutions. Increasingly, psychotherapy approaches are being put to the test and are being held accountable for claims of effectiveness. Along with assessing the general and specific effectiveness of psychological approaches with a variety of issues, researchers have attempted to understand the factors that account for client change across psychotherapy models or approaches.

This research has shown some interesting and encouraging results.[1] First, psychotherapy in general is largely effective at helping people with a variety of symptoms and issues. Second, some therapy approaches seem to be more effective than others in assisting with specific types of issues. Third, certain factors common across approaches seem to account for most of the change that occurs in psychotherapy. In particular, the most potent factors accounting for client change are (a) the client and his/her life circumstances, (b) the quality of the relationship between the client and therapist, (c) the therapist's techniques, and (c) the client's sense of expectancy and hope. The first two, client circumstances and the therapist-client relationship, seem to account for most of the change.

Spiritually-oriented psychotherapy utilizes these same factors and includes an emphasis on incorporating spirituality for therapeutic value. Specifically, spiritually-oriented therapy invites us to explore our definitions of and experiences with spirituality. The focus is on acknowledging and embracing the Energy and events in our lives that bring feelings of centeredness and inner peace as well as clarity of perspective. In short, spiritually-oriented therapy intentionally invites us to notice and access our Real Self, which acts as a conduit to the deep pool of knowing and presence that is Spiritual Energy.

In this chapter I discuss key themes and aspects related to how psychotherapy can support healing and growth, and the ways in which spiritual practice can aid and facilitate the psychotherapeutic process. The emphasis is on how you can utilize psychotherapy to reclaim your Real Self.

A Collaborative Team

What are the key elements of a healthy client-therapist relationship? Why and how does the therapeutic alliance assist people with finding their own inner wisdom? How can you have a strong and productive alliance with your therapist?

For many years I have given students in my "Introduction to Counseling" classes the opportunity to attend counseling sessions with a therapist of their choice and then write a paper about the experience. It has been an amazing privilege and an extraordinary learning opportunity for me to read over a thousand of these papers. Over and over students write about the importance of the relationship with their therapist. Students consistently equate success in therapy with how well their therapist does across several key points and questions. For example, does their therapist show sincere interest in them? Do they feel genuinely cared for by their therapist? Does their therapist listen accurately and non-judgmentally? Does their therapist understand their concerns? Are they and their therapist able to form a shared understanding of the goals and direction of therapy? What happens when there are challenges to their therapeutic relationship?

In support and confirmation of these student views, research has concluded that, generally speaking, if the therapeutic relationship goes well, the therapy goes well. The complex nature of this relationship boils down to some key elements: trust, respect, nonjudgmental acceptance, feeling heard and understood (accurate empathy), clear expectations of the professional relationship and of boundaries, shared focus and goals, match between therapist conceptual intentionality and client needs, shared motivation for progress, encouragement of risk-taking, and ability to work through challenges to the relationship. When these key elements are in-place, the relationship is healing and allows for an environment where other important factors can have an impact (i.e., client variables, therapist technique, and hope).

The essence of a productive therapeutic alliance revolves

around the ability of the client and therapist to form a team to collaboratively address issues and concerns that are important to both. This collaborative team, which I call *Level One Therapeutic Alliance*, is foundational to success in therapy. When one person truly and deeply listens to another and a collaborative team is formed, it is a gift of immeasurable magnitude to both.

A healthy and productive client-therapist relationship is a safe place where we can quiet down and look inward, look and listen to our Real Self, and be open to spiritual nourishment. We are able, for example, to reflect on our conflicted and painful feelings and begin to make sense of our needs and difficult and confusing experiences. A strong therapeutic alliance provides the kind of validation that was missing in many of our childhood and family experiences. It helps us develop a coherent narrative or understanding of our current and historical experiences, thoughts, feelings, and behaviors.

The therapeutic relationship creates a transitional space where we can explore parts of ourselves and try out new behaviors as we prepare to try them out with others in our life. Thus, it also provides an experiential model of how to have an authentic relationship with another person. Ideally, the therapeutic relationship offers an invitation for clients (and therapists) to embrace their Real Self and to have a genuine encounter. This deceptively simple process sets the stage for how much and how quickly therapy will be helpful to clients. It sets the trajectory for the entire change process.

So, how can you have a strong relationship with your therapist? The place to start is by choosing an effective therapist who can be a good match for your style and needs. No one therapist can be effective with all types of issues and all clients. An effective therapist, then, is one that matches your needs and expectations and has skills in addressing your issues. Thus, it is often helpful to choose a therapist through a referral rather than from a list of insurance providers. Referrals can come from health care providers that you trust or from others who know you well.

Once you begin therapy, you can do your part to develop a healthy relationship with your therapist by actively engaging in the process. The alliance grows when you open-up and take risks. Despite being intuitive, therapists can't read your thoughts or really know you unless you allow them to. Engage in the process and share of yourself in the relationship, including any ambivalence about the process. It truly takes both you and your therapist to make it work.

Sometimes people tell me about how they don't trust or feel comfortable with their therapist. If you find yourself in this situation, I strongly encourage you to do something about it, rather than sitting in silence while your experience suffers. In general, the first action I suggest is to speak directly to your therapist about your concerns. Most competent therapists won't get defensive and will value the feedback. Finding an assertive voice will be viewed as a healthy step, one that will eventually strengthen the therapeutic alliance. If your therapist gets defensive, by minimizing or blaming, find another therapist! The therapeutic alliance is too important to the entire change process to be compromised.

Self-Awareness

Self-awareness is a foundational aspect of how psychotherapy helps in general, and of how it assists people specifically in re-discovering their Real Self and a connection with Spiritual Energy. As I have discussed previously, life tends to come at us in an assaultive fashion, knocking us off center and away from our Real Self and from our spiritual grounding. As we move away from the guidance of Spiritual Energy and our Real Self, we likely will become reactive and lose touch with our core sense of integrity.

Unfortunately, it is so easy to operate from a reactive position, acting with little reflection or awareness of the emotions, thoughts, and agendas that impact our moods and behaviors. Once we become reactive, we can act in ways that we may regret: expressing anger inappropriately, getting caught up in other people's dramas, responding to or initiating excessive flirtation with others, etc. At some point we step back and question our motives and choices, and sometimes realize that we need to fix the mess that we inadvertently created. So, how do I stop acting reactively? The answer to that question begins with self-awareness.

Most of us have been taught to not be self-centered or self-absorbed. We have received messages about not focusing too much on our own needs and about engaging in activity-oriented ways of operating in the world. In other words, we are taught to define ourselves by what we do rather than by who we are, by *doing* rather than *being*. The problem, of course, is that we move away from listening to the grounding Energy and intuitive knowing of the Real Self.

A funny, yet true, example of this occurred to me during the first year of my doctoral training. I was very happy to be in my graduate program and extremely busy with all the various tasks. On any given day I was: taking classes, working with clients at the university counseling center, teaching undergraduate classes, studying, and working as a research assistant. Some days I would get so busy and task-focused that I would *forget* to go to the bathroom. On several occasions while teaching large classes, I suddenly became painfully aware that I hadn't relieved my bladder in many hours. I became literally bent over with pain and urgency. I had been ignoring my body and all internal cues until I couldn't wait one more moment! I had to excuse myself and hurry down the hall to the bathroom. It was not only embarrassing, but startling in terms of the degree that I was out of touch with my body and inner experience, focusing almost exclusively on the external world and tasks. And, it happened on more than one occasion.

While most aspects of life encourage us to be externally focused, self-awareness is about tuning in and listening to your inner experience, including your emotions, thoughts, and body sensations. Psychotherapy provides an opportunity to slow down and turn your awareness inward. Spiritually-oriented psychotherapy, in particular, invites you to increase your awareness of how Spiritual Energy is available in the present moment when you are awake to it.

Psychotherapy provides a vehicle to process life and all that it stirs up in us. Most of us try, consciously and unconsciously, to tune out our body sensations, feelings, and thoughts that seem threatening to us or our relationships. Therapy invites us to develop a connection with our bodies and our inner experience. This will likely include approaching and investigating anxiety and uncomfortable feelings. Anxious feelings will be a teacher if we listen to what they are saying rather than blindly reacting to them, ignoring them, or acting on them. In other words, reflection on our inner life can provide a rich source of knowledge about who we are and what we may be avoiding; thus, we can increase our ability to thoughtfully choose, not just react.

All behavior serves a purpose and represents an attempt to meet our needs. This simple, yet profound, statement reminds us that all behavior, including seemingly odd and dysfunctional behavior, is

Rick Johnson Ph.D.

purposeful, even if we are not fully conscious of the purpose. In fact, most of us are not very conscious of the emotions and needs that underlie much of our behavior. We all have basic needs for love and belonging, for example. Unfortunately, the need for love (or any need), can prompt us into reactive attempts to attain connection with others, such as caretaking, accommodating, placating, pursuing, and controlling, to name a few.

A very important point to remember is that your needs are not problematic! *It is how you attempt to meet your needs that can lead to difficulties.* Therapy is a place where you are guided inward, to explore and normalize your needs and to understand the various ways you have been trying to meet them. By understanding that your behavior is an attempt to meet a need, you will feel less pathologized and more empowered in your attempts to find healthy ways to meet your needs. For example, it is not wrong or bad to want to be loved. However, when you attempt to meet your needs for love and belonging in unhealthy ways, it can bring great suffering to you and others. Simply put, therapy provides a place where you can increase your awareness of your needs and can find healthy ways to meet those needs.

Similarly, before changing an "unwanted" behavior, it is advisable to understand what the behavior has been trying to accomplish. For example, if a man has been distancing in his relationships, although hurtful and infuriating to his partner, it is quite likely that the distancing behavior has been serving a protective purpose, possibly protecting him from rejection or criticism. Unfortunately, the "protective" behavior ends up bringing more rejection and criticism as his partner becomes increasingly impatient and annoyed with the distancing behavior. Thus, therapy helps increase awareness of the needs, emotions, and anxiety that may underlie and motivate specific behaviors.

We all have certain emotions that are easier for us to access than others. And we all have shadow parts of our personality, which contain denied or disowned characteristics, emotions, or experiences. The emotions that drive reactive behaviors are both complex and conflicted; we have good reasons for avoiding them. We cannot easily acknowledge, understand, or integrate them.

For some people, anger and frustration are the first emotions that they experience, while sadness and shame are less accessible and exiled into their shadow. They may readily blame others and externalize their emotions, especially if sadness, loss or shame is activated. Simply put, people who are *anger-sadness-shame types*[2] are more comfortable expressing anger than they are acknowledging the underlying hurt. They are *externalizers*. They tend to blame others and to look externally for sources of their discomfort.

Conversely, people who are *sadness-anger-guilt types* are *internalizers*. They are more comfortable turning anger inward and blaming themselves than blaming others. When they do get in touch with and express their anger, guilt is activated and triggers them back into disempowered sadness. This is the underlying dynamic of depression and chronic sadness (dysthymia) for many people.

Thus, for many of us conflicted and painful emotions tend to be pushed out of awareness into our shadow. We live within a muted and truncated range of emotions, consisting of the most acceptable and easily accessible ones. Deviations from the emotional range are regulated by rigid rules and harsh beliefs. For example, "crying is a sign of weakness," "anger is dangerous and unacceptable," and "I will lose control if I get in touch with my long-avoided pain." Therapy provides a space where we can engage with and express thoughts and emotions that are more difficult for us to access. Therapy provides us a chance to break the rules that limit our ability to be more emotionally free. It offers a place to become more aware of and integrate the shadow parts of our personality.

A common technique that I use to help clients increase self-awareness is a mindfulness-oriented body scan. This exercise first asks clients to bring their awareness to their breathing, then center their awareness on their body and any sensations they may experience. I assist clients (or teach them how to do it on their own) to go through each part of their body and invite and notice any feelings and sensations. Along with grounding themselves to a greater degree in their bodies and learning from their emotions and experience, they often describe a sense of *spiritual stillness*, which then opens their consciousness to the wisdom and clarity of their Real Self.

Insight

Many of us have very little insight into the sources of our difficulties. As I have mentioned, often we avoid thinking about painful memories and minimize the impact of past experiences on our current life. Yet, we can't seem to talk ourselves out of feeling unhappy and, at times, uncomfortable in our own skin. We continue to periodically feel, for example, anxious, depressed, angry, lonely, unlovable, inadequate, and unworthy. Therapy provides a forum to understand the various forces, past and present, which impact our moods and behaviors.

Where and how do we develop beliefs about ourselves and about what we can expect from others? For the most part, the answer is that we learn who we are and what to expect from others from our significant relationships, past and present. Significant relationships typically include: (a) past experiences with family members growing up, (b) past experiences with intimate partners, friends and others, (c) current experiences with members of one's family of origin, and (d) current experiences with intimate partners, children, friends and others, including therapists. One of the ways psychotherapy is helpful, then, is when it facilitates insight into the links between these various relational systems and experiences.

Linking, as it is called, fosters insight into the patterns and themes that occur across relationships in a person's life. Often, we first learn about who we are in our families. In our families, we: (a) have significant relational experiences, some of which can be traumatic, (b) play certain roles (e.g., caretaker, pleaser, rebel, etc.), and (c) learn how to protect ourselves relationally (e.g., to be a "good boy/girl"). These experiences, roles, and protective strategies tend to then be replicated or reacted against in relationships outside of the family, often beyond our conscious awareness. Many of us feel a sense of relief when we begin to understand the reasons why we feel and act the way we do.

Insight helps us put the pieces of our life together in our mind, to re-claim *lost* parts of our relational history. Trauma, in particular, is associated with gaps in memory. Therapy provides a space where we can make connections between events and develop a *coherent narrative* of our life story. Insight helps provide a conceptual framework that we can use to make sense of ourselves and our life.

Thus, insight and linking tend to help us answer *why questions* about ourselves and our life. It helps us understand why we react in patterned ways to certain circumstances and triggers. Insight also helps us re-claim our relational life story and begin to take ownership for our lives.

Rick Johnson Ph.D.

Re-Experiencing Relational Dynamics

As helpful as insight can be, we often need something more to assist us to overcome patterned feelings and behaviors. Lasting change tends to occur on an experiential level. In other words, we must *experience* change, in addition to developing an understanding of why we react the way we do. Where can we experience change? One very likely and important place is with a therapist.

As I have discussed, relationships, especially with parents and significant others, teach us about ourselves and what we can expect from others. From our relationship experiences, we form *relational blueprints*, including patterned roles and styles of relating to others. We bring these relational expectations and styles into therapy. To greater or lesser degrees, we transfer expectations of how we have been treated in the past onto our therapist. We also use the same protective strategies (i.e., caretaking, accommodating, externalizing anger, distancing, etc.) with our therapist that we use in other areas of our life. And, therapists bring in their own expectations and strategies into the process. (Hopefully the therapist has engaged in some meaningful exploration in therapy of his/her own relational blueprints and corresponding issues.) When the client-therapist relationship reaches the level that the dynamics that are occurring between them can be usefully and intentionally processed, they are operating on what I call *Level Two Therapeutic Alliance.*

Although these dynamics occur in all therapeutic relationships to some degree, some psychological approaches do not value or recognize these dynamics as useful to the therapy process. In these cases, client and therapist consciously or unconsciously choose to not notice or address these dynamics. Or, they get acted-out by client and therapist in ways that can become detrimental to progress in therapy. At the very least, therapists that don't usefully address the dynamics between client and therapist are missing the wonderful and typically profound opportunities for experiential change that a Level Two Therapeutic Alliance generates.

So, how is the re-enacting of relational dynamics therapeutic for you? If your therapist is able to intuitively or intentionally respond to you in ways that challenge your problematic beliefs and expectations, a *corrective emotional experience* occurs. That is, as your therapist responds in ways that challenge your unhealthy expectations, you begin to experience healing related to your original wounds (i.e., the experiences that created your problematic expectations in the first place). You then have an opportunity to experientially disconfirm your erroneous expectations of yourself and others. This typically leads to greater freedom of choice; you are less likely to respond in automatic and rigid ways in an attempt to protect yourself. You are able to generalize the experience with your therapist to others in your life.

A typical scenario that many clients experience with their therapists, for example, is expectations that their therapist will be critical or rejecting, largely based on their past experiences with their parents and/or significant others. Clients with these issues will eventually *test* their therapist to see if their therapist will respond in ways that are similar to these important others. They may even try to bait their therapist into a critical response, for example, by being critical or rejecting of their therapist. When clients and their therapists can usefully talk about these dynamics and the underlying motivations, healing and growth occurs.

The essence of *testing* is about healing on an experiential level. We all have a Real Self that wants to heal and to embrace health. When we are out of touch with our Real Self, our attempts to test and heal often become a *repetition of familiar and fear-based experiences.* Conversely, as therapists respond correctively to our testing behaviors, we regain some connection with our Real Self. We start to understand that we don't have to blindly act out old patterns; we can instead take intentional risks to embrace the life-affirming aspects of our relationship with our therapist. We experientially learn, for example, that not all women will be rejecting and that not all men will be critical or cross our boundaries, etc. This experiential learning softens our hearts and the rigidity of our beliefs and our protective strategies. As the strength of our pathogenic beliefs and fear-based inner-voices recede, the voice of our Real Self naturally emerges.

In this way, Level One and Level Two of the Therapeutic Alliance support each other. As you develop greater trust and comfort with your therapist, you are more likely to test and to take risks within the therapeutic setting. As you usefully process and experientially challenge these *transference dynamics,* the strength of your therapeutic alliance increases. You then learn to not only trust the relationship with your therapist, but to also trust yourself. With your Real Self in charge you can take greater ownership for your needs and find healthier ways to meet those needs.

New Relationship with your Real Self

A positive and corrective therapeutic relationship, then, supports you in developing a new relationship with your Real Self. As a colleague of mine said recently, the primary goal of therapy is to help people be led by their core Self, their Real Self. How does therapy help the Real Self lead the way? An integration of various theoretical approaches, especially Internal Family Systems (IFS) theory (discussed in Chapter Two), provides a useful framework to further understand this process.

Many contemporary personality theorists argue that the personality is made up of multiple parts. In IFS theory language, there are *managers*, *exiles*, *firefighters*, and the core *self*. For most of us, our conscious sense of ourselves is as a manager: we define ourselves by our actions and our attempts to control our worlds. We spend most of our time surviving, planning, organizing, mastering, and striving; this is our basic sense of ourselves. Once in a while (the frequency and intensity typically depends upon the level of unresolved trauma in a person's background), we become aware of some painful and disavowed emotions or memories that are normally exiled out of awareness (e.g., shame, hurt, self-criticism, anger, dependency, etc.). When these intolerable emotions or memories are accessed, our firefighters jump in to protect us from these painful feelings. Firefighters may include addictions, dissociation, rage, withdrawal, and other strategies designed to quickly return our painful emotions and memories to their place of exile, that is, out of our conscious awareness. Then, our managers can regain control and send us back into a task-focused way of operating.

Thus, for many of us, our consciousness is filled with our managers, and to a lesser extent, our exiles and firefighters. And, we have only a faint awareness of the existence of our core self, our Real Self. Therapy is productive when it helps us *remember* to access our Real Self and when it fosters a new relationship between the various parts of our personality.

Specifically, your Real Self is accessed by remembering and noticing its existence: moments when you feel calm, centered, competent, capable, clear, and courageous. This is a place where spiritually-oriented therapy can be of great assistance to you. Spiritually-oriented therapy encourages you to access Spiritual Energy in your own life-affirming ways. You can also experience

Rick Johnson Ph.D.

and access Spiritual Energy during sessions. For example, I find that helping clients to attend to their breathing in the present moment is often the quickest way to begin to re-connect with Spiritual Energy. Quieting down the external and internal noise allows clients to listen to their intuitive knowing, to be filled with spiritual presence. Therapists can support this process by inviting their clients to turn inward and attend to their hearts and to utilize their reflective and spiritual practice. Over time, what emerges is ever stronger glimpses and clarity about what is life-affirming and growthful.

Each part of the personality serves a purpose, but the Real Self needs to guide the way, to be the leader. Exiles need to be heard, for example. Painful memories and emotions need to be expressed. This is often referred to as *inner child work*, when we have experienced trauma in childhood (i.e., verbal, physical, or sexual abuse or neglect). The inner child needs to be seen and heard or it will become increasingly frantic in its attempts to be noticed. These frantic attempts can include uncomfortable feelings leaking out at inopportune times and our consciousness being flooded with painful images, dreams, and physical sensations, to name a few. Rather than our firefighters automatically jumping in with their oftentimes destructive protective strategies, therapy can help us learn to pause, what Tara Brach refers to as *"the sacred pause."*[3] By pausing right after being emotionally activated, we can then notice and access our Real Self and have our Real Self develop a healing relationship with the other parts, including the exiled inner child. Our Real Self can thank the firefighters for bringing the situation and associated need to protect to our awareness, and then ask the firefighters to step back while our Real Self takes over.

Typically, facilitating a relationship between your exiles and your Real Self involves allowing your exiles to speak while you are consciously operating from your Real Self. An analogy to this process is a parent listening to and comforting an upset child. I often have clients engage in some mindful breathing to bring their Real Self to their conscious awareness, then visualize their inner child in a state of pain. Then, the Real Self asks the visualized child what he/she is feeling, wants to say, and needs. The Real Self listens, comforts, and soothes the child, rather than exiling him/her.

Again, a personally-defined spiritual practice can support this process and provide access to soothing Energy. This *self-validation* and *self-soothing* is crucial for us as we heal from trauma and regain a sense of balance and personal power. In this way, the relationship between your Real Self and your exiles begins to resemble your relationship with your therapist: both are based on validation, love, respect, and empowerment.

When you learn to access Spiritual Energy and your Real Self, your Real Self leads more and more of the time. Your managers still keep you task-focused, but the fear-based motivations are softened and the joy of the tasks can be experienced. Your exiles still alert you to pain and unresolved experiences, but they are much less frantic; your exiles are feeling validated and soothed. There is also a greater freedom of emotional expression. Your firefighters still alert you to times when you feel vulnerable and need protection, but the urgency and destructiveness of their alerts are reduced and they more readily step back and allow your Real Self to handle the situation; your firefighters trust that your Real Self is capable of addressing your concerns. In general, life-detracting behaviors are replaced with life-affirming choices based on the wisdom and guidance of your Real Self.

Rick Johnson Ph.D.

Embracing Inner Health

Inner health is always trying to emerge. Our Real Self is always trying to help us. Psychotherapy is most helpful when the process encourages us to recognize the face and voice of health. Therapy assists us the most when it utilizes our strengths, calls upon and facilitates our capacities, and utilizes our struggles as opportunities to learn, grow, and become more whole.

Trust your impulse; don't act reactively on the impulse. Health often emerges in your consciousness through emotions, thoughts, and behaviors that you first experience as an impulse. You might experience, for example, an impulse to connect with an intimate partner or to engage in some form of addictive behavior. Neither of these impulses is problematic per se. Impulses reflect an attempt to meet a need or resolve a conflicted issue. Specifically, the need to connect with an intimate partner could reflect an underlying sense of loneliness and a desire to be loved and accepted. The addictive behavior could be a repetition-compulsion related to unresolved past trauma. That is, you can be driven to engage in behavior in an unconscious attempt to heal and resolve experiences where you have become emotionally stuck. In this way even seemingly "bad" or unproductive behavior is often an attempt (albeit largely unconsciously) to heal and grow.

Consider the example of John, a 45 year old married man who entered therapy after his sexual addiction was revealed. He was meeting women on the internet and engaging in sexual liaisons, after which he experienced excruciating shame and guilt. Yet, he was unable to control his impulses or change his behavior. His wife, of course, was horrified by his behavior, viewing his actions as a personal attack on her as well as moral weakness in him. His impulse had to be bad or wrong, right?

Shortly after starting therapy John revealed that he repeatedly experienced sexual abuse from a teenage male babysitter when he was 6-8 years old. His sexual addiction and underlying impulse could now be understood as an attempt to repeat and fix his unexpressed and shame-based trauma history. Health was trying to emerge through the impulse to engage in addictive behavior.

Therapy provides a place to explore the underlying needs and motivations of an impulse, rather than blindly act in automatic and patterned ways. Once underlying needs and motivations are understood, this insight can be put into action through self-awareness. In John's case, his insight allowed him to develop a greater understanding of why he was acting in these ways and what was really at stake—he could work to heal his unresolved sexual abuse history or keep traumatizing himself and others through his addiction. His behaviors needed to change, while the underlying impulse needed to be honored. When he was able to become aware of his impulse in the moment, he could pause rather than act mindlessly and automatically. He was able to experience the impulse, then pause and connect to his Real Self. His Real Self provided the wisdom into what could effectively and responsibly meet his underlying needs without addictive behavior. He also developed a mindfulness-based spiritual practice that supported his ability to pause and embrace healthful Energy in his life.

John's story provides a wonderful example of the power of health in your life. Health is always trying to emerge in your consciousness, even in seemingly odd or problematic ways. Struggle tells you that something isn't right. Therapy can provide an opportunity to view and re-experience your struggles as an attempt to define yourself, heal unresolved issues, become more whole, and meet your needs in healthy ways.

Rick Johnson Ph.D.

Embracing Relationship Health

Although the therapeutic relationship provides an experiential model for a healthy relationship, the client-therapist relationship is a transitional one. And, although it should be an
authentic relationship based upon genuine caring, it is also a relationship that is ethically and clinically limited by professional
boundaries. Thus, you need to transfer the learning and experiences from your therapist to other significant relationships in
your life. Healthy relationships are where lasting change occurs:
with therapists, with your Real Self, with Spiritual Energy, and
with significant others. As therapy assists you in remembering
and re-connecting with Spiritual Energy and your Real Self, you
begin to naturally discriminate between life-affirming and life-
detracting relationships and experiences. Your Real Self provides
the barometer and guide in this journey.

Therapy provides a place where you can notice how you
feel and ask a variety of questions about the various relationships
in your life. For example, do you like how you feel and who you
are when you are in your relationships? To what degree are your
relationships life-affirming or life-detracting? Do you feel a sense
of personal integrity vis-à-vis your relationships? What are your
experiences telling you about what is right for you and who you
want to be?

As you evaluate your relationships based on the inner
knowing of your Real Self, you will become increasing clear
about what is life-affirming for you and the ways in which you
need to grow. With your Real Self in charge, you will naturally
begin to notice and value what is healthy and life-affirming. You
will also find more effective ways to meet your needs and address
your underlying impulses to heal and grow. As you internalize
the healthy aspects of your relationship with your therapist, you

will be open to and choose life-affirming relationships, where your soul can be nourished and sustained.

Utilizing Spiritually-Oriented Psychotherapy

The most potent predictor of change in therapy is the client. You have the most power to change your life and to embrace health; and spiritually-oriented psychotherapy provides an avenue to do just that. The following is an example of someone that utilized the power of spiritually-oriented psychotherapy to reclaim her Real Self, transfer her emerging health into sustainable relationships, and transform her life.

Joan entered therapy when she was 38 years old, suffering from debilitating bouts of depression. She was unhappily married with 2 kids. Her husband did his best to stop her from having friends outside the family. She was isolated, disempowered, and self-hating.

The first, and central, aspect of Joan's therapy was forming an authentic and healthy relationship with her therapist. This was not easily accomplished. She did not readily trust others, especially men, and her self-criticism often prevented her from believing that she was worthy of another person's attention and care. Slowly, she formed a therapeutic team with her therapist, which became the "sacred space" where she could process her enormous pain and gain the support she needed to risk taking ownership for her life.

Joan began to reveal a history of horrific physical and sexual abuse at the hands of various relatives, including her father. Insights related to the abuse and other dynamics in her family of origin helped her understand why she developed such low self-esteem and tended to protect herself by distancing and self-punishment. These insights also made her difficulties with trust, including with her male therapist, make a lot more sense to her. She began to test her therapist to see if he would be there for her, or if he would abandon or abuse her, as others in her life had done. Over time, Joan and her therapist collaboratively addressed her transferred expectations that he would abandon and hurt her, which led to numerous corrective emotional experiences.

Insights that linked her past experiences with current relationships also led to increases in her self-awareness. Typically, she felt "numb" if triggered emotionally. Over time, she began to experience her emotions and became much more aware of her inner experience. She began to realize that she would "flash" to a memory of abuse from her childhood, right before she went numb. Slowly, she was able to pause before she "tuned out." She was able to "stay in her body" for longer periods of time.

She also started to have experiences of being calm and centered, moments of clarity and peace. Her therapist often invited her to notice these moments, and to understand their importance for her healing and growth. She began to be interested in various forms of spirituality. She joined a church, where people were openly inviting to her. Her prayer-life brought more moments of peace and support. She indicated that on several occasions the "Holy Spirit" filled her with self-acceptance and love. She began to intentionally access Spiritual Energy regularly through prayer and mindful breathing, which she experienced as a loving and guiding presence in her life. She reasoned that if she could be loved and accepted by this Energy, then she must be worthy of being treated better than how she was treated as a child and how her husband treated her.

Joan became increasingly in touch with her Real Self. She had more frequent mental and physical sensations of her "true self" emerging. The impulses that emanated from her Real Self were about creativity, exploration, and freedom. She had dreams and visions of herself as a butterfly emerging from a cocoon. Joan wanted to express herself in ways she had never allowed herself before. She became aware that she wanted to go to college. She wanted friends. She wanted to pursue creative arts. And, she wanted her husband to support her in her growth and healing.

Unfortunately, he was threatened by her changes, and tried to suppress her emerging health. Again and again, she tried to reason with him and include him in her process. Eventually, she realized that she would not be able to be healthy if she stayed in the marriage. Despite being nearly incapacitated with fear, she maintained connection with her Real Self and drew strength from Spiritual Energy, which provided her with the guidance and courage to proceed on her path of health.

After a difficult and painful divorce process, Joan emerged with her integrity intact. She had refused to engage in conflict-drama with her ex-husband. She pushed for a fair and reasonable settlement, despite his attempts to sabotage her efforts.

Although rocky times occurred, Joan's self-esteem continued to improve. She continued to take risks by pushing herself to meet people, and build upon her life-affirming friendships that had formed over the past year. Much to her surprise, she met a man who really wanted to know and support her. She tested him repeatedly. Her Real Self knew what she really wanted and deserved in a relationship. She opened her heart to his genuine kindness and love, leading to many corrective experiences. She was breaking all her childhood rules. She was listening to her Real Self. She was accessing Spiritual Energy, which nourished her soul. And, she embraced the health of her life-affirming relationships. She truly blossomed with the guidance of her Real Self and nourishment of her spiritual practice.

Rick Johnson Ph.D.

Final Thoughts

Psychotherapy can be a vital and vibrant aspect of personal growth and healing. It assists you on multiple levels, most foundationally by providing a relationship that supports all the elements of the change process. Psychotherapy is most helpful when it is in-line with your inner wisdom and supports your impulses for health and healing. In short, therapy is most effective when the process encourages you to notice and activate your Real Self as a guiding force. Once your Real Self is accessed, you naturally become discerning in your life. You evaluate your life structures and determine the ways you need to grow and the changes you need to make. Real Self-defined spiritual practice, which supports life-affirming choices and activities, is an invaluable part of the process. Spiritual Energy is a healing and growthful presence, which reminds you of who you truly are and of your potentials for being. Psychotherapy that supports engagement with your Real Self and utilizes personally-defined experiences with Spiritual Energy provides you with tremendous opportunities for attaining sustainable health.

So, notice those glimpses of something greater than your ego-driven personal story. Take Spiritual Energy's invitation to be filled with clarity and purpose. Engage in your spiritual practice to open your heart and nourish your soul. Your Real Self is ready to lead your life.

NOTES

CHAPTER THREE

1 *Face of God*, a poem from *Sandstone Monastery*. Reprinted by permission of the author.
2 I John 4:13, *New International Version*.
3 Thich Nhat Hanh, *Living Buddha, Living Christ*, p. 203.
4 Joan Halifax, *The Fruitful Darkness*, p. 13.
5 Wisdom 1:7, *New American Bible*.
6 I John 4:16, 18, *New International Version*.
7 Mathew 11:28, *New International Version*.
8 Mathew 18:20, *New American Bible*.

CHAPTER FIVE

1 Marianne Williamson, *The Gift of Change*.

CHAPTER SIX

1 Michael E. Kerr, *Chronic Anxiety and Defining a Self*, p. 46.

CHAPTER TEN

1 Mark Hubble, Barry Duncan, & Scott Miller, *The Heart and Soul of Change*.
2 Edward Teyber, *Interpersonal Process in Psychotherapy*.
3 Tara Brach, *Radical Acceptance*.

SELECTED BIBLIOGRAPHY

Bass, R. *The Book of Yaak*. Boston: Houghton Mifflin, 1996.

Bohart, A. C., & Tallman, K. *How Clients Make Therapy Work*. Washington, DC: American Psychological Association, 1999.

Bowlby, J. *A Secure Base*. New York: Basic Books, 1988.

Brach, T. *Radical Acceptance*. New York: Bantam Books, 2003.

Bowen, M. *Family Therapy in Clinical Practice*. New York: Aronson, 1978.

Cameron, J. *The Artist's Way*. New York: Tarcher/Putnam, 1992.

Dreher, D. *The Tao of Inner Peace*. New York: HarperCollins, 1990.

Gibran, K. *The Prophet*. New York: Alfred Knoff, 1983.

Greenberg, J. R., & Mitchell, S. A. *Object Relations in Psychoanalytic Theory*. Cambridge, MA: Harvard University Press, 1983.

Halifax, J. *The Fruitful Darkness*. San Francisco: HarperCollins, 1993.

Hanh, T. N. *Living Buddha, Living Christ*. New York: Riverhead Books, 1995.

Harvey, A. *Journey in Ladakh*. New York: Mariner, 1983.

Hollis, J. *Finding Meaning in the Second Half of Life*. New York: Gotham Books, 2005.

Horney, K. *Our Inner Conflicts*. New York: W.W. Norton, 1945.

Horney, K. *Neurosis and Human Growth*. New York: W.W. Norton, 1950.

Hubble, M. A., Duncan, B. L., & Miller, S. D. *The Heart and Soul of Change*. Washington, DC: American Psychological Association, 1999.

Rick Johnson Ph.D.

Ingram, C. *Passionate Presence.* New York: Gotham Books, 2003.

Kasl, C. *If the Buddha Got Stuck.* New York: Penguin Books, 2005.

Kerr, M. E. *Chronic Anxiety and Defining a Self.* The Atlantic Monthly, 1988.

Linehan, M. M. *Skills Manual for Treating Borderline Personality Disorder.* New York: Guilford Press, 1993.

Loy, D. *Lack and Transcendence.* Amherst, NY: Humanity Books, 1996.

Magid, B. *Ordinary Mind.* Boston: Wisdom Publications, 2002.

Minuchin, S. *Families and Family Therapy.* Cambridge, MA: Harvard University Press, 1974.

Moore, T. *Care of the Soul.* New York: HarperPerennial, 1994.

Rogers, C. R. *On Becoming a Person.* Boston: Houghton Mifflin, 1961.

Schnarch, D. *Passionate Marriage.* New York: W. W. Norton, 1997.

Schwartz, R. C. *Internal Family Systems Model.* Oak Park: IL, Trailhead Publications, 2001.

Steindl-Rast, D. *Foreword* in *Living Buddha, Living Christ* by Thich Nhat Hanh, 1995.

Sullivan, H. S. *The Interpersonal Theory of Psychiatry.* New York: W. W. Norton, 1953.

Suzuki, S. *Zen Mind, Beginner's Mind.* New York: Weatherhill, 1973.

Teasdale, W. *The Mystic Heart.* Novato, CA: New World Library, 1999.

Teyber, E. *Interpersonal Process in Psychotherapy, 4th ed.* Belmont CA: Brooks/Cole, 2000.

Tolle, E. *The Power of Now.* Novato, CA: New World Library, 1999.

Tsu, L. *Tao Te Ching.* Translated by Gia-Fu Feng and Jane English. New York: Vintage Books, 1989.

Warren, R. *The Purpose Driven Life.* Philadelphia, PA: Running Press, 2003.

Weiss, J. *How Psychotherapy Works.* New York: Guilford, 1993.

Williamson, M. *A Return to Love.* New York: HarperCollins, 1992.

Williamson, M. *The Gift of Change.* New York: HarperCollins, 2004.

Wright, A. *Sandstone Monastery.* Portland, OR: Wijiji Publishing, 2004.

Acknowledgments

To begin, I want to thank my wife, Joellyn, and our two wonderful daughters, Madelyn and Mia. Without your love and support, this book would not have been written.

To my parents, siblings, extended family, and friends, thank you for providing me with the support I need to embrace my Real Self—the journey continues.

To my mother, Bernie Johnson, Ed.D., and friend, Robin Bagai, Psy.D., thank you for your tireless support in helping me with all aspects of this process, including editing and finding the voice and audience for the book.

Thank you to my friends and colleagues in the Buddhism and Psychotherapy Study Group, which meets at the Zen Center of Portland. Many of the ideas in this book percolated in our wonderful and nourishing discussions.

To my friends, colleagues and students at Portland State University, your support has given me the motivation to carry this book through to its conclusion. Your warmth and sincere interest have inspired me.

Lastly, I want to extend a very special and heart-felt thank you to the clients in my private practice. It is an honor to be with you on the journey of discovery, healing and transcendence. Your courage and impulses for health are the essence of this book.

You are invited to continue engaging with ideas in this book at:

RECLAIMINGYOURREALSELF.COM

For more information about the author, visit:

RICKJOHNSONPHD.COM